At Home in the Group Home?

An Insider's Look at Congregate Care

By Youth Communication

Edited by Al Desetta

YOUTH COMMUNICATION

True Stories by Teens

At Home in the Group Home?

EXECUTIVE EDITORS
Keith Hefner and Laura Longhine

CONTRIBUTING EDITORS
Kendra Hurley, Nora McCarthy,
Sheila Feeney, and Rachel Blustain

LAYOUT & DESIGN
Efrain Reyes, Jr. and Jeff Faerber

COVER ART
YC Art Dept.

For reprint information, please contact Youth Communication.

ISBN 978-1-935552-20-8

Second, Expanded Edition

Printed in the United States of America

Youth Communication ®
New York, New York
www.youthcomm.org

Catalog Item #CW15-1

Dedication

This is the first in a series of 15 books by teens about their experiences in foster care.

Most of the stories originally appeared in *Represent: The Voice of Youth in Foster Care*. Youth Communication founded that magazine in 1993 to help reduce the stigma of being in care, and to give young people a way to share their experiences, and their suggestions for change, with peers, parents and foster parents, and the adults who run the system.

Since 1993, more than 300 teens have written for the magazine. Tens of thousands of teens and staff have read their stories in more than 100 issues. Thanks to the courage of those teens— and many others nationwide—the voices of youth in care can no longer be dismissed.

But it took more than courageous young people to make that happen. It took money and vision. The Child Welfare Fund gave the first grant for *Represent* in 1992, and continued to provide significant support for 15 more years. We are deeply grateful to the Child Welfare Fund and its director, David Tobis.

**We dedicate this book to the anonymous donor
who created and supported the Fund
and made it possible for the teen writers to tell their stories.**

Table of Contents

Contents

Contents

Girls Like Me

> Rana appreciates the chance to live with girls she can relate to.

Five Steps Behind

> The staff at Kareem's group home didn't prepare him for life on his own.

Man With A Plan

> When a fellow resident ages out into homelessness, Michael resolves to make a plan for himself.

Missing My Old Group Home

> Six months after leaving his group home, Max finds himself doing something he never expected: missing the place.

FICTION SPECIAL: Lost and Found

Using the Book

Introduction

In *At Home in the Group Home?*, teens write about the pros and cons of group homes, and how living in congregate care has changed their lives. These 21 true stories don't sugarcoat the difficulties of group home life, but they also show how group care can be a successful alternative to foster homes or traditional families in some situations. These stories are ideal for discussions with teens and staff about what makes group homes work and how they can be improved.

In the opening story, Tamecka Crawford fears going into a group home because she had been warned about them by her brother: "He said the girls would test me, that I would fall into a clique, and that I would be very lonely."

Yet Tamecka soon finds that the other residents "didn't care what type of home I came from or whether or not I was a 'problem child.'…I stayed there for six months and in those six months I grew as a person. I went through bad times and good. The most important thing was that I didn't go through them alone. The staff always gave me a shoulder to lean on, which made me feel like I belonged."

Angela R., in "The Rules Make Me Feel Safe," has a similar experience. Going into a group home was "a nightmare come true," yet she flourishes under the rules and structure.

"I was given chores and a bed time," she writes. "For the first time I ate meals at the table, with other people. Whenever I needed someone to talk to, staff were there most of the time. For the first time I was being listened to, without getting hit if someone didn't agree with me."

When Rana Sino tells people she lives in a group home with 11 other girls, they automatically assume she's miserable. She admits that she could complain on and on about the mood swings, the stealing, and the fights.

"But the truth is," Rana says, "the biggest part of me is happy to be where I am. I consider the girls my sisters, not only because we all live in the same house, but also because we share similar problems."

The writers are equally honest about the shortcomings of group homes. They describe teasing, scapegoating, drug abuse, and theft by residents. And relations with staff aren't always ideal. Kareem Banks believes he was failed by the adults in his group home.

"It was like having blind or dead babysitters," he writes. "No one ever talked to me about going to college or vocational school, how to have a career, how to rent and keep an apartment, how to resolve conflicts with people, or even how to cook a hamburger all the way through."

Yet, more often than not, *At Home in the Group Home?* is about teens growing and maturing through the group home experience. Karol Kwiatkowska learns that it's more important to be herself than to act wild and rebellious to fit in with cliques. Sharif Berkeley overcomes his fear of gay people when he lives in a mostly-gay group home. Eric Edmonson benefits from freedom and opportunities he didn't have living at home.

And after aging out, Max Moran has a shocking realization: "I never thought I would say this in a million years, but sometimes I do miss my old group home." The experience, he writes, "has made me strong, and today I'm not afraid of anything."

While there is much debate over the value of congregate care, many teens will continue to be placed in group homes. These compelling stories show how teens and staff can make them work.

In the following stories, names and/or details have been changed: *Sober in a World of Unreality, No One to Trust,* and *Jasmine, the Scapegoat.*

Justin Riley

My First Day

By Tamecka Crawford

My brother Damon was placed in a group home for about a year. Although he got into fights and complained, it really did him some good.

Still, Damon always used to tell me how miserable I would be if I ever went into a group home. He said the girls would test me, that I would fall into a clique, and that I would be very lonely.

I never imagined I would go to a group home, but there were a lot of problems in my family. I was tired of feeling like I owed them something every time they did something for me. The social workers didn't want to put me in a group home, but it couldn't be avoided.

So, one day in October, I was driven in a big, blue van from the foster care office to a group home in a different neighborhood. I was very scared, since this was my first time away from family.

There was a girl and her baby in the van, along with two child welfare workers. The girl was bragging about how many group homes she had been in. She was talking about how people steal your things. She stared at me and noticed I wasn't saying anything. Maybe she saw the scared, anxious look on my face, or maybe she just knew I had never been in a group home before.

I was staring out the window, trying not to let her get to me, when she suddenly pulled on my shirt and said rudely, "Nobody will like you if you be yourself, you can't be quiet like that. They'll try to test you or think you're a nerd."

I thought about what she said and, without a word, turned back and looked out the window.

I really didn't know what to expect. I am a very family-oriented person. I couldn't even begin to imagine what my new family would be like. I'd heard how much I could benefit from living in a group home, but also that it could destroy my life. I decided to calm down and take it one step at a time.

All kinds of things were running through my mind as the van drove along. I was imagining white ladies in uniform, "enforcing the rules" with whips and white gloves. How would the other girls take to me? Would I eat beans every night for dinner?

We finally drove up in front of the group home and the butterflies hit me hard. I thought I was going to throw up. As I got out of the van my legs started to lock. I could feel the tears coming but I didn't want anyone to see, so I quickly wiped my eyes and walked to the door of my new home. Somehow I knew I was doing the right thing.

I was greeted by a nice short lady, Ms. Rivera. (In my mind I was saying, "Thank God she's not white." Even though I didn't grow up around racism, I felt most white people didn't understand where I was coming from.)

Anyway, the social worker who drove with me in the van gave Ms. Rivera my papers, wished me good luck, and left me.

I followed the counselor up some stairs, through a hallway, and into an office.

The house seemed cold (not weather-cold, but it didn't feel homey). Ms. Rivera asked me a few questions and did an inventory of my belongings. I asked her about the rules and regulations of the house.

She said most of the girls stayed to themselves. She said we were allowed to take a nature walk each week. Everybody had a chore to do twice a day. We had group therapy every Monday, she said, and then two girls dodged into the office and asked, "Are you done yet so we can talk to our new roommate?" They seemed happy to see me and showed me our room.

The two girls talked to me for hours. Wanda, a short, light-skinned girl with a squeaky voice, had been there for a while, but Tiny, a tall, slim girl, had just arrived earlier that day. They told me how I had to learn things for myself. (I thought that was very nice for them to say, since people usually want to give you their opinions of how things are.) They told me a little about how the rest of the house looked and the other girls' names.

It was an all-girls home with 12 residents. All the furnishings were made of white wood. Everybody had a twin bed, a

We finally drove up in front of the group home and the butterflies hit me hard.

dresser, and a night table. The room was pretty nice. Of course I had to add my touch to my side of the room, and then it would look much better.

I couldn't fall asleep because I still had butterflies in my stomach. I was excited about meeting the other girls and at the same time scared because I always kept to myself. They might ask me questions about my mom or dad, or even ask why I was there. These were all questions I wasn't ready to answer, and they might judge me right away.

The morning finally came. I just lay in bed listening to the rest of the girls getting ready for school. Then it sounded like all the girls were in my room, trying to check me out.

They pretended not to pay me any attention as I sat up from under the covers with my pillow over my head. I wanted to see their faces before they got a chance to see mine. When I peeked, there were only four or five girls in the room.

Wanda introduced everyone. They all said hello and welcomed me. I couldn't tell if they actually meant the welcome or not. Nobody started asking me questions, which meant that everyone stayed out of each other's way. I laughed to myself as I lay back down, thinking that this might work out after all.

As a staff member made lunch for Tiny and me, I checked out the house. It was a two-story house with a basement. There were four bedrooms, a bathroom, and lounge on the top floor, and one bedroom, an office, a half-kitchen, a bathroom, and a living room on the first floor.

In the basement there was a laundry room, a kitchen and dining area, another office, and a bathroom. It was a nice-sized house for 12 girls, which meant that everyone had room to breathe. After switching from my family to these strangers, I needed all the space I could get.

By dinner time I was sort of relaxed because I had met all the girls and no one asked me anything except my name and age. They didn't care what type of home I came from or whether or not I was a "problem child."

The staff always gave me a shoulder to lean on.

At dinner there were two tables of six. One big pitcher of Kool-Aid for each table, and everyone had to stand up by the kitchen area to be served. I was very happy that dinner wasn't beans. The food was actually pretty good.

Everyone was telling the staff what happened that day. It seemed like they were arguing, but that was just because everyone was talking at once, saying pass me this, pass me that.

After dinner the girls had to do their chores (cleaning the

bathrooms, kitchen and dining room, laundry room, etc.). I was going to be assigned a chore the next morning, so I laid back and enjoyed the free time while it lasted.

After an hour or so of just hanging around the house or watching TV with everyone else, it was time for bed. The butterflies were finally gone. I had lived through my first day in the group home without anyone giving me the nasty look or starting a fight, like my brother had said would happen. It was funny, too—I didn't even miss not being at home.

I stayed there for six months and in those six months I grew as a person. I went through bad times and good. The most important thing was that I didn't go through them alone. The staff always gave me a shoulder to lean on, which made me feel like I belonged. I found a new home and a new family.

Tamecka was 18 when she wrote this story.
She later attended college.

Melissa Rivera / Percyell Smith

At Home in the Group Home

By Taheerah Mahdi

If you came to my group home, you would see girls everywhere. Some would be doing their hair. Others might be screaming out a song or sleeping in their room. You might even see one girl fight another for some stupid reason.

When I first got there, I didn't want to know any of them. I thought they were going to be wild and mean. To my surprise, they weren't. Instead, in my group home I finally felt like I could fit in. I found out that I could be myself and that was OK.

That was a big relief, because in my foster home I felt like I had to be the child my foster mother never had. When I went into foster care, I wanted to keep doing the things I did when I was at home, like cooking for my sister and myself and washing my clothes. My foster mother wanted to do that for me. I understood that she meant well, but she didn't understand that I had many reasons for wanting to take care of myself.

At home, I used to take care of my family by washing and cooking and my mom treated me more nicely when I cleaned the house. She would say things like, "Good job, I'm proud of you," and, "I couldn't get a better cleaner than you." That made me feel like I was wanted and that I was kind of special to be able to get my mother to smile.

When my foster mother tried to do everything for me, I felt unneeded and unwanted. And I couldn't seem to let her get so close that I'd let her do things for me. That seemed too intimate to me.

When I let my foster mother know that I could take care of myself, she was angry. She told

The best thing about my group home is that I feel that I'm not so different from the other girls.

me that as long as I was under her roof, then she was the adult, not me. She made it seem like I was a troublemaker and I wasn't listening to her. But she wasn't letting me learn her ways at my own pace.

I didn't want to take my foster mother's power away, but I wanted her to understand that it was hard to learn her ways of living. I was already dealing with a lot inside when I came into care. Maybe if she'd let me be, over time I could've learned to let her take care of me.

Soon after I came into her home, though, she showed me in a more serious way that she was willing to put her own needs before mine. When she started dating a new boyfriend, he tried to molest my sister and me. We were so scared that I started to keep a knife for protection.

Eventually I told my foster mom about her boyfriend, but she wouldn't believe me. She acted like I was trying to hurt her, and instead of protecting us she protected herself.

After that, she would go to her room and lock the door whenever she was in the house. She made me feel like I was the problem, not her boyfriend, and that there was no one to trust out here in the world. I came into foster care to escape that kind of abuse, and her reaction made me feel that everywhere I went, people would always try to hurt me.

Soon my sister and I got moved to the group home. Honestly, it's not always easy being here. Sometimes I have to deal with a girl not liking me, and with knowing that the staff are not my best friends. But most of the time I feel protected there. I know that the residents are looking out for me.

One time when my sister had an asthma attack while I was asleep, the girls were very kind. They made sure that my sister was OK. I realized that the girls cared about my sister and me.

But the best thing about my group home is that I feel that I'm not so different from the other girls. Once I was talking to one of the girls in the house and she said, "I'm afraid of trusting people. It's been a while since I said that I trusted a person."

She made me feel that she came into the system feeling the same way I did. I didn't feel so alone anymore.

All of the girls in my house are struggling with something similar. Once when I was talking to this girl about how it feels better to be in here than to be out there not knowing where to put your head down, she told me that it was OK to let out all of my feelings, and that this place isn't bad when you get used to it.

Like the other girls, I feel like my staff also help me feel comfortable being the way I am. My relationship with the staff isn't close. I can't seem to sit down with any of them and talk about how I feel. I want to be closer to the staff and to other people, but as a little girl it seemed that the more that I tried to get close the more I got rejected at home. When I tried to get to know my mother, she pushed me away and made me feel that the best thing to do was to stay to myself.

Now, in the group home, I act how I used to when I was home: seen but not heard, quiet unless I want to have a little fun and turn on my radio and dance around. Sometimes I just need to be alone, and I sit outside and look at the water. That makes me feel that I can let out whatever is on my mind without being interrupted.

Still, I think living in my group home is slowly helping me get a little more comfortable getting close to people. Now I cook for myself sometimes, and I have to cook for my chore. When I cook for the girls at my house, I feel good knowing I can still take care of other people, but I can also let the staff do it sometimes.

And there is one staff that I feel I can trust. She's an Indian lady who has long, straight hair, small, dark eyes, a round cookie face, and a nice, comforting smile. I got to trust her one day when I felt sad and I sat next to her. The first thing that she said

It's not always easy being here. But most of the time I feel protected.

was, "You hungry?" I didn't know what to say. Then she said, "Eat cookies. You skinny." I thought she was a nice lady who didn't speak too much English.

After she gave me the cookies, I watched her as she walked around the house trying to sweep. Then she said, "You sad? Come eat some soup I made." I started laughing because her soup was salty. Then she sat next to me and said, "It's not so bad here, it grows on you."

When she told me that I felt like she understood how I felt. Since then I haven't talked to her so much, and I'm not too close to her, but I feel that when she needs me and when I need her, we'll be there for each other.

Taheerah was 16 when she wrote this story.
She later attended college.

Eduardo Marquez

Get Me Outta Here!

By Miguel Ayala

When I entered my first group home, I was scared. I thought that a group home was like was an orphanage, and I half expected nuns to come out with rulers and start busting ass.

There were no nuns, but I could tell right away that my group home was trouble. I knew it from the way the residents sat making noise on the house porch while smoking cigarettes with complete disregard for the neighborhood or house rules. (One of the rules was, "Do not sit in front of the house.")

Still, I thought at first that I'd do OK there. The residents and I would watch TV, lift weights, and have friendly boxing matches. But it was through those boxing matches that everyone found out I was soft and that I would not fight back even when I was getting hit. Soon I was getting choked out by residents and was getting my stuff stolen by them as well. It made me feel like I was at home getting abused by my mom, and I was very scared.

After a while I was thinking, "Why do I have to live with a bunch of teens who bully me? Why can't I be in a foster home? Why won't someone adopt me, take me into his or her home?"

Even after all I've been through in a family environment, I still need to be in a family setting where I can get love from adults. The love you get from a parent is different from the love you get from a child care worker or group home staff. In my group home, I was not being hugged and kissed goodnight like I was used to, and that made me sad.

I knew I couldn't live with my mom and that was cool, but I didn't think I got the attention I needed for my depression, anger, or suicidal thoughts in a group home. And the drugs, fights, and stealing that went down every day made me feel like I was about to explode. I often wonder whether, if I lived with a family, I could have avoided the time I AWOLed for an entire summer, or whether I would not have attempted suicide three times.

Maybe with a family I wouldn't be under so much stress, and the attention I would get would give me a sense of worth. Maybe being with a small family would help me cope with my problems and help me feel normal.

Again and again I told my social worker I wanted to get put in a foster home or be adopted. She understood why—she knew how the residents teased me and how once they trashed my room and destroyed everything I had, including my cell phone. Still, all my social worker would say was that they were working

Maybe with a family I wouldn't be under so much stress, and I'd get the attention I needed.

on finding me a better home. Hearing that response all the time began driving me mad.

Sometimes, to calm down, I imagine a life away from the group home. I imagine getting adopted into a home that has only the good things of all the places I've ever lived. I picture a white picket fence, a two-story house, and a yellow door with three mirrors on each side. I imagine wind chimes and a porch. I imagine a mom and a dad, a dog, and two other kids—a boy and a girl. I picture us all in the house, preparing Sunday dinner.

Maybe it wouldn't be like that. Maybe my social worker thinks that if I got in a foster home I'd be disappointed there, too. But I still think I'd be better off with a family than where I am now.

Miguel was 20 when he wrote this story.
He later earned his GED.

Terrell Perkins

The Rules Make
Me Feel Safe

By Angela R.

Going into foster care was a nightmare come true. My mother had always made it my worst fear. She told me horrible things about foster care. I was more scared to be separated from her than anything in the world.

The first time I went into foster care I was 8 years old. My mother and I were living in a homeless shelter at the time. She would always pick me up from school in the afternoon.

One day she didn't come for me. I sat in the usual spot in the lunchroom, where all the other kids were getting picked up. After a while I had a feeling that she wouldn't be coming for me. The school called my mom's social worker, who came from the shelter to pick me up.

The social worker brought me back to the shelter. By this time I was crying hysterically. I waited in the social worker's office for what seemed to be hours, but my mother never appeared.

This wasn't the first time my mother had left me alone, so the people from the shelter were fed up with her. Eventually the social worker called someone from the foster care system to pick me up.

I went into a foster home. A few months passed, then my father got out of jail. He found out that I was in a foster home and began to visit me. I was so happy that I didn't care about my father's drug addictions. I also completely blocked out the fact that he had molested me when I was 7 years old. All I saw was my chance to get out of foster care and to have a real family.

It took a while, but the foster care system finally let me go back to live with my father and his new wife.

My father tried to force a mother-daughter relationship on his wife and me too fast. It ended up causing friction. We were very spiteful towards each other, because we were both jealous about my father's attention. He also began molesting me again. I felt dirty and I hated myself. I began to hate the rest of the world for all of my problems.

My father also verbally abused me. I got called "white trash" and "an ungrateful little #@%$&^." Once my father broke my nose by throwing a keyboard in my face.

I was doing horribly in school. I never did any work. I was getting below 40s on all my tests. I got hit every time I brought home my report card. My father signed me into a mental hospital when I was 14. It was the same hospital where he went to drug rehab. I was put in the teenage ward because I was depressed and not going to school.

The night before I went to the hospital, my father told me not to tell anyone that he had sexually abused me. We both agreed that it wasn't the sexual abuse that made me depressed, so I wouldn't tell anyone. I really wanted to believe that the abuse wasn't making me miserable, although it was. Looking back, I feel sad that my parents brainwashed me into saying what they wanted me to say and feeling what they wanted me to feel.

Being in the hospital was safe and relaxing. It was unlike anything I ever felt before. I got up enough nerve to tell my roommate what my dad was doing to me, but I made her promise not to tell anyone. My roommate told me to tell my therapist, but I wouldn't listen. I began to feel depressed again, because I knew that I would have to go back home in a couple of weeks.

Being away from my family made my whole life easier.

Every day in the hospital we had community meetings for everyone on the floor. We discussed our problems and told the rest of the group what was going on in our lives. You could say anything you wanted to say in the community meetings.

One girl began to talk about her brother sexually abusing her. I knew that if I talked about my situation, I would be safe. I wouldn't have to worry about my father coming after me. I didn't care about him abandoning me either, because now I had people on my side who were stronger than he was.

At one community meeting I got up enough courage to come out with the abuse. At first I didn't think I'd be able to do it.

My arms and chest went heavy when the staff asked if anyone had something else to say. I couldn't raise my hand or open my mouth to speak. My body went numb.

Somehow I managed to raise my hand. When I was called on and before I could speak, I broke down and cried. I had never really cried about the abuse before. I threw the words out from my chest, crying hysterically like a baby.

It was the hardest thing I have ever had to do, but it changed my life. I decided not to even try to work things out at home. I agreed to be put into residential treatment.

Being away from my family made my whole life easier. I still had the depression and self-hatred, but at least I now had staff and therapists who would listen to me.

I was given chores and a bed time. For the first time I ate meals at the table, with other people. At home I always ate dinner alone, which was usually something that I could pop in the microwave, because my parents were never there.

When I needed someone to talk to, staff were there most of the time. For the first time I was being listened to, without getting hit if someone didn't agree with me. When I lived with my parents, they were too busy telling me their problems. They thought that I shouldn't have problems because I was just a kid.

My group home gave me a lot of structure, which is what I needed.

I adjusted to the rules well, because I liked the way the rules made me feel safe. I never had any structure in my life before. My group home gave me a lot of structure, which is what I needed.

Now, a lot of times I feel like breaking the rules because I've had a lot of structure for the last year. Sometimes it feels like the staff enjoy putting me on restriction or taking money from my allowance. It's like they get off on controlling my life. I have to admit that this is how I feel when I don't get my way. But I know that the staff are enforcing the rules because they care.

I'm not gonna lecture you about how you should respect staff and follow all the rules. I just feel that foster care can be a good experience for some kids. The rules are designed to protect you and give you structure. If you have a problem following those rules, it's probably because you weren't getting enough structure at home.

If I didn't go into foster care, I would still be back home, living miserably with my parents. I would be much worse off because I wouldn't have dealt with my problems. I would be praying for my father to have an overdose, because back then that was the only way I saw out of my pain.

I'm much happier living in foster care. Even if I had the chance, I would never go back home to my family. The group home I'm in now is my real home.

Angela was 16 when she wrote this story. She graduated from the high school at her RTC and went on to college.

YC Art Dept.

The Adventure Begins

By Delicia Jones

When I first got placed in the system, I spent my night driving around in a van with a guy I didn't know who seemed to enjoy taking people from their families. At about 5 the next morning, I got to my new home. I felt all choked up, like my whole world had been shattered, like it was a delicate glass sitting on some edge and now it had finally fallen off. I was in a group home.

On the way to my new room, I got kind of scared because I saw a sign that said "Jewish Board of Family and Children's Services." I knew I wasn't Jewish. Then a staff took me up a staircase that said "Boys' Staircase," and I wasn't a boy.

When I got to my room, there were two other people in there. One of my roommates had her head covered and the other one was just about bald, so I really believed staff had me on the boys' floor. That night I cried myself to sleep with the feeling that I might have a heart attack from all the pain in my chest.

The next morning I was woken by four girls in towels conversing about me and some other new girl. They were saying, "Neither one of them is pretty." I was already upset, and they weren't making it any better.

When I sat up, they all got quiet. After about 30 seconds of awkward silence they each came over and introduced themselves. Some of the girls gave me nasty looks and that made me feel a little out of place, but there were others who made me feel like I might be OK there. Later one girl told me, "Most of the girls here are nice, they just have to get used to you."

One girl that sticks out in my mind from my first days in the group home was the first girl to bring me to her room and explain how things worked. She would say stuff like, "That girl is cool, but don't tell her anything you wouldn't want anyone else to know, 'cause if you get into an argument with her she'll throw it back in your face in front of everybody."

That girl was the first person I felt comfortable around. Anytime I had a problem I would go to her and we would cry together, like the time I found out a friend of mine got shot. She helped me calm down and made me feel like I wasn't alone. She hugged me and rocked me back and forth, telling me it was going to be OK.

It felt good to know that I had so many people trying to keep me on the right track.

Eventually I got close to staff, too. From the staff I had three mothers and one dad. It felt good to know that I had so many people trying to keep me on the right track.

One particular staff member would give me one hour every Friday night to talk about what was on my mind. I think I would have made some wrong decisions without that hour.

After we had our talks, she would walk me to my room,

tuck me in my bed, give me a kiss on the cheek, and tell me she loved me. I didn't hear that very often, but when she said it, I felt special.

Delicia was in high school when she wrote this story.

Percyell Smith

I'll Take the System

By Erica Harrigan

Last year I went AWOL from the Wayside Home for Girls, a group home in New York City, because it was a bad place for me.

I thought the staff acted like they hated to come to work, just wanted to get paid, and didn't care whether the kids behaved. With the staff not taking action to keep the place tight, the kids ruled the campus.

I hated it there. Kids picked on me constantly. I lived for my day pass when I went to my aunt's house. My aunt gave me good advice and was loving toward me.

But some weekends, staff shut the whole cottage down if one person did not obey the rules. Home visits and day passes were out of the picture for everyone.

When the cottage was on lockdown, it hit me hard. My blood would boil and I'd get tense thinking about having to stay inside my room all day. No TV or radio playing, just plain silence. I had a single room, so I had to lay there and look at the four walls. It was my personal cell.

One time I figured I might as well get in trouble for something I'd done. So I trashed the place and fought the staff till they threw me in my room and locked the door behind them. I banged on the door till I fell on the floor sleeping.

The following day I was taken out of class and told that I was going to the hospital because I'd attacked a resident and a staff. Next thing I knew, I was weeping inside a big red van on my way to Holliswood Hospital. I couldn't take it anymore. As soon as I got back to Wayside, I AWOLed.

Ever since my mom started using drugs, when I was 8, I'd wanted to live with my aunt, so I went to her house. But living with my aunt made me feel depressed.

I felt like I was Cinderella and my cousins were the two evil stepsisters. I had to do everyone's laundry—about eight big black garbage bags a week—and never even got a thank you. My cousins also made me their dodger. I would go back and forth to the store for them. They would even wake me out of my sleep to go to the store.

I started to realize that I needed a few things only the system could give me.

I felt I had to do what they wanted because I was a runaway. Plus, if I didn't, my cousin would talk about me and embarrass me in front of everyone. I would get upset and pack my things to leave, even though I had nowhere to go. Those nights I would sleep on the stairs. I didn't mind. When I lived at home with my mother as a kid, she'd get angry or be out getting high and I'd end up sleeping in the stairwell all the time.

I was hoping that, by being kind, I could change the way the way my family treated me, but now I thought my family would always be the same. I also started to realize that I needed a few things only the system could give me.

In the system, I was on medication. Living with my aunt, I kept flipping out when I ran out of medication. I didn't have a Medicaid card, so I couldn't get new pills unless I went to the emergency room. I also didn't get therapy, and I wasn't in school because my aunt couldn't legally register me.

When I went AWOL, I thought all I needed was my family's love. But living with my aunt, I realized I needed stability, therapy, and an education, too. Finally I decided to go back in the system.

I'd heard rumors from other girls that Wayside was closing down, but I didn't believe it one bit. Then I called Wayside on the phone and found out the number was disconnected.

For a moment I felt free. Then I wasn't sure where to go. I feared that if I went to the courthouse and turned myself in, a judge would send me straight to jail. But finally I went to my agency and asked for a placement. They told me my case was closed because I'd turned 18. Then they asked me, "Who are you connected to?" I said, "My aunt," and they told me to go back there.

I couldn't believe I was being sent back to the home I'd just left. I felt tears drop on my cheeks. I wanted to cry and beg them to send me anywhere but there. I feared that if I told someone at ACS (the city foster care agency) why I didn't want to return to my aunt's, they'd take her kids. (They'd already investigated her once.) I'm not that grimy that I'd bring ACS to her home. So I just brushed the tears off and went back.

It was just like before: My aunt didn't help me get into school, get therapy, or arrange Medicaid so I could stay on my medication. I started to believe she took me in for the SSI money she got for me. My aunt has always cared a lot about me and I love her, but I was fed up with my so-called family.

After four months I went to live with a friend, but if we disagreed about something, she'd threaten to kick me out, saying, "You could get out, this is my house." Then, after a month, she made a move on me.

Finally, I called up my law guardian and told her what happened. I wanted her to send me anywhere else. She told me to go to the ACS office and they would take me back.

When I got to ACS, a lady told me my case was closed. I was lost. I didn't know what to do. I had no place to go other than my aunt's, and I'd decided that I wouldn't go back there if my life depended on it.

I begged the lady to help me. She suggested I go to Covenant House, a shelter for teens, which accepted me as a runaway. Then, after about a week, ACS placed me into care again and sent me to a transitional group home.

> **The staff are real. They don't bite their tongues and they tell it like it is.**

The staff was cool, but the environment was not. There were a lot of pimps who hung around there and I just didn't feel comfortable. Pimps kept on threatening me, saying, "I'm going to put you in stilettos" and things like that. By that time, I was really stressed. I'd been to four different places and none of them seemed like a place where anyone was looking out for me.

Finally, I got transferred to a small group home called 50th Street. For the first time I feel safe and calm. It's the best place I've ever been. I think I was sent here to find myself.

The area is peaceful. Nice and quiet block, no traffic. Kids play in the yards and people are respectful to each other. It's a nice spot to sit and chill with friends. Around the corner are stores, the library, the train station, and restaurants.

This group home is kind of like a family. There are only two other girls and two staff on each shift. Because it's small there's not much drama. The staff speak to me on topics a mother would usually talk to a daughter about, and they treat me like they'd treat their own children. If I need guidance, we click, and they don't get on me too much. The staff are real. They don't bite their tongues and they tell it like it is.

The staff have taught me how to budget my money and cook. They exercise with me and go out to eat with me as well. We also read books and magazines together. I am doing much better than before. I am finally stable, but I still have to work on my anger and communication skills. I talk about that in therapy and with my staff.

After a long search, I'm glad I've finally found somewhere to stay where I feel like I'm moving forward in life.

Erica was 19 when she wrote this story.
She later got married and had two children.

Nelson Choi

All the Lonely People

By Karol Kwiatkowska

I'm wandering aimlessly around my group home. My next stop is the living room, where 11 happy-looking faces are playing board games and cards. Envy knocks in my head and my mind starts screaming, "I too want a friend!"

Feeling miserable, I turn and go to my last stop—my bedroom. I'm sick of looking at the same four walls of my room every day, but I can't think of anything better to do. I sit on my bed and think, "I read all my books, I did all my homework, and I'm sick of writing in my journal. All my friends live far away, and besides, they have their own lives and don't understand what it's like to live in a group home. The staff here are busy with their work and I'm not one of the 11 happy faces in the living room. I'm sick of it all! I'm lonely! And hey, here comes my friend envy."

For those of you who live in a group home, you probably

know that feeling. It feels like a very cloudy, dark day. It's not raining, but it's really quiet and it looks like a powerful thunderstorm is about to hit. It happens when you're feeling down or bored and you start wondering why you're living in a group home. On days like these you don't want to wake up and do anything because there's nobody or nothing you have to turn to. You feel like a worse feeling is going to hit you any moment. You feel incredibly alone.

I interviewed some group home teens and they all agreed that loneliness is a big problem in group homes. "When a lot of kids come they don't really know where their mother, father, or siblings are," said Natasha Springle, 19. "They don't have friends, so loneliness is like the biggest problem."

My friends from my old life didn't really understand what I was going through.

Angelina, 18, agreed. "Group homes make you depressed. People there don't help you get your life together. Loneliness is a big problem."

Tyelisha Washington, also 18, said she often felt lonely. "I don't have any close friends in this group home," she said.

Teens in group homes have many reasons to feel lonely. For one, it's hard to be separated from your family. Before I went into a group home, I was with my brothers and sisters 24-7. I had fights with my siblings now and then, and sometimes I couldn't stand them, but once I went into the system and was separated from them, I felt like someone had ripped out my lungs. A part of me was missing. It was incredibly painful.

Many girls in my group home feel like they need to have boyfriends to not be lonely. Dian, 20, a college student and former group home resident said that she feels lonely when she doesn't have a boyfriend. "I feel disconnected," she said.

Angelina said, "Sometimes when I'm not with my male friend I feel lonely. When I don't spend time with him or if he gets mad at me, it feels bad."

But if their boyfriends let them down, that makes them feel even worse.

Christie, a girl in my group home, was this type of girl. She wasn't close friends with any of the residents. Her boyfriend was her main friend in the world. Then she and he had problems. They broke up, and Christie lost her only friend. For several days she looked miserable and didn't talk to anyone. Things might have been easier if she had made other friends besides her boyfriend.

But the politics in a group home can be difficult to deal with and make you cautious about having friends. You might be different from the other girls because of your clothes or your attitude. Also, being shy might affect you. You might see the other residents getting along and having fun with each other and feel scared to go up to them because you think that they'll make fun of you. Or they might actually make fun of you. That can lead to feeling very alone.

Many of us in group homes can't trust each other. When I first got into the group home, I was very naïve. My roommate asked me, "Can I borrow two of your CDs?" I said, "Sure, go ahead." Guess what? I never saw the CDs again. I was angry, but I learned not to trust just anyone in my group home.

But sometimes we in foster care have trouble trusting even the trustworthy people. Many of us got into foster care because people who were supposed to protect us didn't, so now it's hard to trust anyone. As a result, friendships in group homes usually happen slowly. "It may take a person seven to eight months to say that they trust their friend," Tyelisha said about group home friendships.

But let's say you finally do meet that wonderful friend in your group home. You stop feeling lonely. Then one of you gets moved.

That happened to me. Daniella was my best friend. We did a lot of stuff together like talking, laughing, and going places. For the time she was my roommate, I never felt lonely. Then guess what happened? She was moved from my group home and I went back to being lonely again. I tried to make friends, but it wasn't the same. I missed Daniella.

I tried to turn to my friends from my old life, before foster care. But they didn't really understand what I was going through living in a group home. I started spending a lot of time alone—reading, watching TV, and listening to music. Luckily, I didn't turn to anything negative to take my pain away.

But a lot of people in group homes do start dangerous habits when they're lonely or depressed, like using drugs and alcohol.

Natasha, 19, said, "With loneliness, you do turn to things like drinking and smoking." Dian stated, "When I used to feel lonely I never turned to a specific person. It was sex, weed, cigarettes, alcohol, or drugs. Sometimes a guy, if I had one."

In the long run, some of these things can make you even more depressed.

Many of us in group homes can't trust each other.

Some people really never get close to anyone else in the group home. They build this wall around them and they tell themselves not to trust anyone because they were hurt before and are scared to be hurt again. Those people become isolated. Although they may seem like they don't want friends, I think they're actually lonely and would love for someone to break down their walls.

Karol was 18 when she wrote this story.

Gabriel Appleton

Trapped!

By Mariah Lopez

Being transgendered isn't easy, especially when you're living in a straight group home and you're the only one. But first, let me tell you what a transgender is. Yeah, I know, the first thing that pops into your head is a man with a sex change and a dress. Wrong! A transgender is someone who lives his or her life as the opposite sex. It doesn't mean that they have a sex change—that's a transsexual.

I'm a guy but I've felt like a female my whole life. And when I dress the part, I look a lot like a female, too. I can even get numbers from guys (although I always tell them right then and there that I'm a guy).

I know a lot of people are uncomfortable with who I am, but I hope the fact that I'm transgendered doesn't stop you from reading more. After all, you're learning, aren't you? So let me continue. I'm 14 years old. When I was 6, my grandmother (who raised me) told me I was a boy. Until then, I didn't know that. I felt and thought like a girl. I walked with my chest sticking out and I liked to wear my hair in a pony tail. I even liked dressing in girls' clothes.

When I was growing up everyone knew me and my family, so they didn't bother me. But when I went into foster care at the age of 8, it was a different story.

The first group home I was in, where I stayed for three years, was terrible. So were a lot of other group homes I've been in. But they weren't terrible at first, because my grandmother was still alive and when anything happened to me, she would report the staff to the social worker and complain.

But after she passed, things got worse and worse. I had at least two fights a day. The boys used to do stupid things because I was gay, like throw rocks at me or put bleach in my food. Once I was thrown down a flight of stairs, and I've had my nose broken twice. They even ripped up the only picture of my mother that I had.

In my group homes, being transgendered was always a problem.

Often the staff were bad, too. If I had a fight with one of the staff earlier in the day, they would start conversations with the other boys in the group home about the argument just to get them riled up. Then the boys would come up to me, challenging me and calling me a faggot. Sometimes the staff would stand there while the kids jumped me. One time a staff member jumped me with the kids.

My grandmother always told me to be myself and be proud. But when these things were happening I didn't know what to do or who to turn to. Most of the time the staff told me the same things.

"You deserve it."

"Oh well."

"Fight back."

"Don't be gay then."

One time a staff member asked me, "Don't you like men beating on you?" Another staff even told me to kill myself to be out of my misery.

When I got to go to my room, I'd just sit there and cry. Or I'd read a book or listen to music to block things out of my head. I slept a lot, too, so that the days would go by faster. I used to get mad and think, "What's so bad about me?" I'd pray and ask God why He didn't make me a girl or a straight boy so I wouldn't have to go through this. Sometimes I would cry all night, asking Him to change me.

But I never really felt I could change. I was who I was. Through all of these things, I had one constant feeling—the feeling of helplessness, that no matter what I did or didn't do, it would always be the same and that somehow it was all my fault.

I stayed at my first group home for three years. Then one day I went AWOL with only three dollars in my pocket and nothing to lose. I just decided that I had to get off that campus. When I got to the train, I talked the conductor into letting me ride for free. And when I arrived in the city, let me tell you, I hadn't been so happy since I don't know when.

I tried to stay at Green Chimneys, a group home for gay and transgendered boys. But they didn't have room for me and I was too young. Eventually I went back into the foster care system. For the next year I bounced around from group home to group home. I always left because being transgendered was always a problem. I knew I'd be bouncing around until I could get into Green Chimneys or until someone opened another group home for gay kids.

There were a few staff and kids who made me feel really good about myself. At one group home the staff taught the kids that they should respect me, and that helped the kids to be more open-minded. I was even able to date openly. But in most of the group homes people constantly harassed me. After about a year I finally got a phone call from my law guardian telling me that I had a bed at Green Chimneys, so I packed my bags.

When I got there, I still couldn't believe it. I finally felt content—I could be myself and unique at the same time. Sure, there are plenty of things that get me plucked (mad) at Green Chimneys. Just living with a bunch of other teens in foster care can be a nightmare (not that I'm always such a little sweetheart myself). But if it weren't for a supportive group home, I'd still be in a very uncomfortable position and so would a whole lot of other kids.

Mariah was 14 when she wrote this story. She became an activist and advocate for queer youth of color in foster care.

Marcus Pierno

Can the Counselors Keep a Secret?

By Anonymous

Have you ever confided in a staff counselor at your group home about your past life, your dreams, or your secrets? When you ask her to keep it confidential, of course she says, "Don't worry. This is between you and me."

But are the counselors really keeping it confidential? That's something we all have to wonder about.

I often suspect that the staff counselors are talking about the kids among themselves after the chief administrators go home. Evening, night, and weekend shifts seem to be the best times for them to go into their offices for their private, "important" meetings.

Ha! Sounds more like happy hour to me!

When I was in a residential treatment center, I never told a staff counselor about my problems. And when I later moved to a group home, I still didn't have faith in trusting counselors—until about a month after I moved in.

My social worker wasn't in the group home that day and I felt depressed. There was no one to talk to because my friends were still at school or work, but I needed to talk with someone. So I decided to give this "trust" thing a try.

I told a staff counselor why I was gloomy. I told her not to repeat my story to anybody, not even to the other counselors. She said, "Don't worry. We'll keep it confidential."

I told her not to repeat my story to anybody.

Later on that evening, the staff had their usual private meeting in their office. Somehow, I felt paranoid. I remembered when I first came to the group home, the kids told me that certain staff counselors gossip about the residents.

When all the counselors got together for their meeting, I waited for a few seconds and then tip-toed down the hall, bent down, and pressed my ear to the door.

Sure enough, I heard my name a couple of times. Then I heard them calling me "a $&%^#," "a dirty stinky bum that doesn't know how to take care of herself," and a "brat who acts like a little baby and is difficult to handle." The "trustworthy" staff member told the other staff parts of the story I told her (she misinterpreted some of what I said), and then they laughed and made fun of me.

You can imagine how I felt.

To this day, the only times I talk to the staff is when I ask for carfare to go to school or work, or when I have to do my laundry.

It's sad to know that if you trust some staff counselors, the next day they might gossip about you like a dog. It's almost like telling your friend a secret and then having her stab you in the back.

If I have anything I need to confide or get off my chest, I talk to my therapist at our sessions. Or if my therapist has left for the day, I talk to my close friends and tell them whatever's on my mind.

So it's not like you don't have any choice but to talk to a staff member when you feel sad and depressed. You can talk to your therapist or to your best friend.

Or maybe there's a staff counselor who you absolutely trust, who won't gossip about your secrets during the staff's happy hour.

The author was 16 when she wrote this story.

Stefan Vaubel

Making It on My Own

By Eric Edmonson

Living without your parents is not easy, especially if you're living with people you don't know. Before I went into a group home, I thought living with eight boys would be tough (especially if you had no idea where they came from). I thought they would think I was soft because I'm only 4' 11", and would try to rough me up. Lucky for me, this wasn't the case.

When I moved into my first group home, I was having many problems with my aunt. I was lazy and I didn't really help her around the house. Not because I didn't want to, but I thought I wasn't being treated fairly. For example, my cousin could watch TV on a school night and I couldn't.

So my aunt decided that she couldn't take care of me anymore. She took me to a foster care agency. This was not the first time I was sent to the agency for being disruptive. There were lots of other times, too.

When she told me I was moving into the group home, I got real scared. You see, I used to live across the street from a group home. I always thought they were uncivilized teenagers because they would smoke and drink and sometimes vandalize property, and I would make fun of them.

Then the tables turned on me. When I first arrived in the group home, I tried to be quiet and not look at anybody. But this was hard because they were being so friendly to me, giving me junk and candy. Then the supervisor came and told me to introduce myself. I told most of the kids my name.

The staff showed me to my room. I wasn't thrilled about sharing a room with a boy I didn't know, but he turned out to be a cool person and a great ballplayer. I also thought that group homes were dirty, but as it turned out my group home was kept very clean.

I used to live across the street from a group home. I always thought they were uncivilized teenagers.

After a couple of weeks, I started getting used to my new home. I went out and played basketball and learned the area better. I also got to know the residents. Some of them were trouble, so I was told to avoid them. I was happy I received allowance, because that was what I missed out on at my aunt's house. I was also allowed to watch TV on a school night. (Now you probably know why I didn't get along with my aunt.)

Even though I was having a great time, there were rules and regulations I had to follow. First of all, I had to keep my room clean at all times. Second, I had to make sure I did my chores after breakfast and after dinner. Next, I had to be home from school by 4 p.m. to do my homework. I was expected to do all my work in school and pass all of my courses. I also had a curfew at night. If I didn't follow these rules, there were consequences for me.

Now, you might think these rules are strict, but they are better than my aunt's motto: "Work first and don't play later until I say so."

Now don't get me wrong—this group home is not peaches and cream. I do have my ups and downs. I get into a lot of verbal arguments over petty stuff, like my chores or the TV. I haven't gotten into any physical arguments because I would probably get hurt (that doesn't mean I wouldn't fight), but no one tries to fight me because I'm short for my age.

I really thought I wouldn't be in touch with my family after my separation from my aunt. Then a week later my aunt called me. She explained why she put me in a group home. She said it would make me a better person and a responsible young man if I could go out and do for myself.

At that time I disagreed with her and didn't want to hear it. Then she told me there was another reason. She said she wanted my mother to come back and take responsibility for me. She said my mother was living the easy life and wanted nothing to do with me. She also said I'm at that point in my life when I need my mother's advice. But I believe that it's too late for that because I'm becoming a young man.

I thought if I held all my feelings from my family, I would be fine. It didn't turn out that way. I had to speak to someone who could tell me why my mother neglected me. So I tried my uncle. He just told me that I was lucky she didn't throw me in a trash can somewhere. That made me sick and angry. So I hung up on him.

I tried other family members, but none of them had any insight. Then, when everything failed, I turned to a resident.

He told me the only way I could deal with my problems was to be mature about every situation. He told me to stop blaming people and take control of my life. Next he told me that people wear masks and you never know who they are going to be, so you have to be responsible for yourself.

That night I thought about what he said, and decided to go

on a home visit with my aunt, something I had neglected to do.

After I went on a couple of home visits, I began to accept that the group home was my second home. I really didn't get to do anything on my home visits, so my weekends were totally boring. The only thing I did was play video games.

I needed freedom and my second home provided this. I also felt that what my aunt said was true. I saw many opportunities for me begin to open up. Like my independent living program said they could get me into college if I continued to do well in school. I also became a better ballplayer, thanks to another resident. Now I can do anything I want on the court, except rebound.

After six months in the group home, I now believe that leaving my aunt was for the better. I was used to relying on her too much. Even though I need food, clothes, and a roof over my head, some things I can do myself to become a grown man.

I also learned not to make snap judgments about people who are in group homes because it can hurt their feelings. Maybe going through a group home is good for people in my position. And if I ever see my mother again, I want her to know that I'm making it on my own.

Eric was 15 when he wrote this story

Santiago Tau

Sober in a World of Unreality

By Charlene Carter

"Hey Sandra, you wanna smoke?" called Tanya, standing in the doorway of the room I shared with Sandra.

"Yeah, but I won't have any money until tomorrow," Sandra said from under the covers.

"That's OK. Do you wanna smoke?"

Sandra got up and got dressed, and they went off in the middle of the night to get a smoke.

Even though I've been living in this group home for a while and am used to hearing conversations like this, they still disturb me. I know what's about to happen. The girls will go get high—probably on marijuana, the drug of choice in my group home—and then get away with it.

But even though they get away with doing drugs and think that they're doing well, I know they're only making it bad for themselves. They're losing their minds and pretending it's all good. I'll hear:

"Maya is freaking out over this boy. That's why she's missing school. She's doing drugs."

"Shane is doing bad in school. She misses so many days and her counselor says that she's going to get kicked out, but she doesn't care. She just keeps doing drugs."

And the worst of it is that those girls who do drugs are the "in crowd." If you want friends, you hang with them. But to hang with them, you're always around drugs.

When I first moved in the group home, I thought that drugs were just a phase the girls were going through. Growing up in the system means living a rough, uncared-for life. The girls in my group home say they do drugs to help them go through those rough times. They talk about how good drugs make them feel. They say that drugs give them strength and help them cope with their emotional problems. But the longer they do drugs, the more it seems like they won't ever be able to stop using, even after the rough times end.

The longer they do drugs, the more it seems like they won't ever be able to stop.

I've seen a few girls try to stop using and, for the most part, they don't make it. I suspect that the drug use will just be another problem that will mess up their lives even after they've left the system.

Five years ago, I knew little about drugs. I'd heard from community counselors about how popular drugs were, but I had never been exposed to them. No one from my biological family did drugs.

All that changed when I was first placed in foster care. I was surrounded by girls who did drugs. I didn't want to do drugs, but I wanted to be friends with those girls. Those girls had a special way about them. They had a special code. They were a team.

They always hung together. They watched the same sitcoms, went to the corner store together, liked the same fashions and styles, and they did drugs together. They had vivid personalities that could not be missed. They lived their lives in the fast lane, they were exciting to be around, and you were stupid not to hang with them.

*I*f you decided not to hang with them or do drugs, those girls made life hard for you. You wouldn't have too many friends, you'd be bored most of the time, and you'd have to face those girls every day not knowing what they would do to you. Anyone who wasn't down with them could take a walk and that was like living your life on a different planet. Those girls sized up everyone who came to the group home. You were either with them or not with them. But hanging with them meant doing drugs and risking getting in trouble with staff, as well as messing up your mind.

I always wanted to be popular and to have lots of friends. I wanted to fit in with everything even if it meant getting in trouble from time to time. I didn't mind telling a small lie or taking some snacks out of the cupboard without permission or even violating curfew from time to time. But doing drugs was too steep for me. For one, I didn't know how to stash a supply and how to get around staff if I got high. These girls were pros and expected you to learn very quickly. But I wasn't very good at lying about something as serious as that.

If you decided not to hang with them or do drugs, those girls made life hard for you.

And mostly, I was totally uncomfortable with the whole idea of taking drugs. I worried about what it would do to my mind and whether I'd be able to stop once I started. I saw the girls in my group home who tried to stop and couldn't, and I'd heard from counselors that it was really hard to stop using once you've started. So I didn't start at all. I decided to try some other avenue to help me cope with my problems. I focused on school.

Still, sometimes it was tempting to join them. I thought that if I did drugs, I wouldn't be alone.

Eventually, I did make several friends in the group home. Some of them did not do drugs and some did. But many of my friends came and left. They either went back to live with their biological parents or moved to another group home, and I had to make new friends.

Making new friends started to become a difficult and tiring task, and I became discouraged. When a new resident came to the group home, she would approach me and ask me if I did drugs. When I told her no, she would become upset with me. I knew that she thought that I was in a position to ruin her plans, and it took time for her to get to know me a little more and believe that I was not a serious threat to her operation.

Then, most of the time, we still couldn't be good friends because I didn't take drugs. Often I'd think about how much easier it would be to make new friends if I did drugs.

Sometimes I'm still tempted, even though I've been around long enough to see the bad side of it. I remember the resident who would come home with eyes bloodshot red. She'd be wobbling and slurring her speech. Other girls would violate curfew or go AWOL just to do drugs. I have seen many of the girls use their weekly paychecks from working at fast food restaurants to buy some marijuana. Whenever they got some change, they'd use it on drugs.

Many of the girls I've met who take drugs think they can stop. They think that drugs are just a temporary habit, something that will help them get through these rough times living in the foster care system. But I've seen how hard it is for them to stop. Some know full well that they have a chance at a good future and they don't want to mess that up, but they still can't stop using.

As for me, it's hard to live here. When I was first exposed to this drug-infested environment I thought that it would go away, but it hasn't. Being around drugs while living in a group home has been a struggle that is overwhelming. It's a sad experience to go through.

Charlene was 19 when she wrote this story. She attended Borough of Manhattan Community College.

Nishan Aznavorian

No One To Trust

By Lenny Jones

In the system, I've learned an important lesson: You can't trust anyone.

I didn't learn this lesson until a few months ago when my phone mysteriously disappeared. I think it happened while I was watching TV in the living room of my group home. Someone must have pick-pocketed me and taken the phone from the lower pocket of my jeans.

I've had things stolen before—my book bag, shirts, hats, undershirts, socks, and the weirdest thing, my boxers! (How low can you go?) But losing my phone hurt me the most.

The stealing didn't just happen to me, it happened to just about everyone in my old group home. Like this kid Scrub. His CD player disappeared, but he was one of the lucky ones (about one in a million)—he got it back. A staff member found it. When it came to my phone, I wasn't so lucky.

It's also funny how the ones who act so cool with you are the ones who will steal your stuff the quickest. I've seen cases where some residents would treat a new jack (new resident, if you ain't down with the lingo) like he was family, just so they could steal his property and the new jack would never know who did it.

I never found out who took my phone (and no, I'm not a new jack, I've been in the system for about a year and a half). The messed-up thing was when I asked my so-called friends if they knew who stole it. All of them suddenly went deaf, dumb, and blind at the same time.

What was funny was that they had me believing we were so cool. We used to smoke weed and drink forties together (things I don't do anymore), but when my phone disappeared, no one knew a damn thing. I posted flyers about it around the apartment, told the staff, asked residents, offered a reward, and still I ended up with nothing.

Telling the truth is not about snitching, it's about respect. I had enough respect for just about everybody in my old group home (except the cook) not to steal their property. All I asked was for a little respect in return.

I guess I had to learn the hard way. I always tried to look at foster care in a positive way, instead of negatively like other people do (people usually think

I've had things stolen before—my book bag, shirts, hats, and the weirdest thing, my boxers!

everything and everybody in the group home is bad). I thought the people in my group home were trying to change for the better. Now I see it differently. I am more easily suspicious of people.

Before this incident, I didn't really care why a person was in care but now I do. Before I thought everyone in my group home was in the system for the same reason I am (family problems), but I finally woke up. Now I realize that some of them were put into the system by the courts for robbery, stealing, drug and alcohol problems, or for not going to school.

It's not so bad having to live in a group home, but the worst thing it is not being able to trust the people there. The only things I can depend on (and it's not too dependable with all these budget cuts) is the roof over my head and the stiff bed I sleep on, and that's all. The rest is up to me.

When I asked my so-called friends if they knew who stole it, all of them went deaf, dumb, and blind.

A good way to protect your stuff from thieves is to keep your doors and closets locked. You should buy lockable chests (a foot locker) if you don't have lockable dressers or closets. Then you should always use good locks. You shouldn't keep your valuables laying around or visible. You should always watch your back.

The only thing I can't understand is why the agencies can't have locks on all the residents' doors, closets, and dressers. It would eliminate a lot of problems and if something disappeared, it would be the resident's fault for being careless.

You should either get to know someone first before you go trust that person, or just keep to yourself. Sometimes you're better off alone because you can trust yourself more than you can trust anyone else.

Lenny was 18 when he wrote this story. As a researcher for travel guides, he has traveled around the world.

Gary Smith

Safety in Numbers

By Ja'Nelle Earle

When I was growing up, I felt like no one loved me. My sister would talk to her friend about how much she hated me and how I was always ruining something. My mother was an alcoholic and sometimes it seemed she talked to me only to tell me what was wrong with me. She would say, "Pick up your toys," or "You never do anything right." She never really told me how proud she was of my schoolwork or how well I did things. I wanted her to encourage me, but I rarely got that.

I guess my mother thought I was a liar, too, because when her husband was sexually abusing me and I told, she didn't believe me. My mother thought I was making up lies to gain her attention, but little did she know it was the cold and ugly truth.

My family's ridicule and my stepfather's sexual abuse made me feel like I was never good enough for anything. I felt like the oddball. I was mad at the world. Why was I born into this type of family? Why couldn't I have been born into a perfect family?

My life changed one day when a police officer talked to my 4th grade class about rape. He told us to make sure we told an adult we trusted if we were ever raped. So I told my 4th grade teacher how I was raped. My teacher called the police, and within hours my sister and I were taken away from my mother. My mother was furious—Child Protective Services was taking us away because of my lie, or so she thought.

When my sister and I arrived at Hillcrest Receiving Home, I was separated from my sister because a psychologist wanted to talk to me about the rape. I answered what seemed like a million questions. Then the psychologist told me I had been molested, not raped.

The new classification did not make a difference to me. All that mattered was that the only home I had known was now considered unsafe for my sister and me. I was given a new set of clothes and I showered and changed. Then I entered a foreign world. A world of children who had been taken away from their families just like I had.

I didn't know it then, but it would turn out great for me. Instead of ridicule, I would find caring people and encouragement in the system. But I wouldn't find it in foster homes or by living with my grandmother. Oddly, I would find just what I needed in group settings—group homes and residential treatment centers.

Hillcrest was a temporary place for abused children until a social worker could find them another, more permanent place to stay. I didn't know anybody, but what I did sense was that no one was going to hurt me or make me feel bad here.

After a day or so, the unfamiliarity of Hillcrest left me feeling lonely, so I requested to be with my sister. My request was filled, but my void was not. She was not happy to see me. The feelings I had of inadequacy and missing love came rushing back to me. My sister's rejection hurt even more because I was away from home and feeling lonely. I thought she was the only person I had. I was wrong. I didn't even have her. But like always, I put it behind me and kept going.

Shortly after, I met a staff named Yolanda. Yolanda was the role model I had always dreamed of. She was smart, pretty, and she liked me. When I was feeling lonely and would cry, she would hug and comfort me. If I wanted to talk, she listened and didn't laugh at what I said. She never ever put me down. There was a time when I felt a male staff touched me inappropriately and I told her. She believed me, which was amazing because my mother didn't believe anything I said. She was everything I wanted in an adult role model, and that is why our friendship grew.

I was at Hillcrest and with Yolanda for about two months when my social worker found a foster home and I had to leave.

A foster home, a family—that worried me. All of my past feelings came back. I wasn't sure what to expect. Would they ridicule me like my biological family had? Would the other kids be able to relate to any of the hard things I'd been through? Would they think I was strange?

At Hillcrest I had been surrounded by people who had gone through the same things as me and that made me feel safe, like I always had someone to talk to. What would it be like to be trying to fit into a family again?

I was in that foster home only one week. It was no bowl of peaches. The foster mother would make me play outside until it was dark and cold. She also tried to force me to eat things I didn't like and she abused the kids.

This may sound weird to people who hate group homes or think that family settings are better for kids, but I really missed Hillcrest. I wanted to go back to that comfort zone badly. After about a week in the foster home, I heard the foster lady spanking the other kids. She told me to behave or she would spank me too. I knew that was good enough reason to leave.

I called my social worker in a hurry, but she told me there was no other foster home for me to go to. I asked her if I could return to Hillcrest, and with a puzzled voice she asked me if I was sure. Maybe she was puzzled because I wanted be in a facility rather than a home with a family. But I thought of some of the people in Hillcrest as my family. When I said I was sure I wanted to go to Hillcrest, she took me back there.

I was excited to be back. I had my old friends and I made new ones. The food wasn't that great and it was still overcrowded, but the warmth heated me up to where I could be happy again. I was out of the cold, cruel world and back into my safety zone. I had that feeling you get when you know something good is going to happen and you stay excited for days.

What I didn't know was that my stay at Hillcrest had to be temporary. I stayed for about another month. As soon as my social worker found another placement for me I had to leave Hillcrest, and this time it was for good. But the thing I remember most is that I found the comfort, care, and warmth I had always wanted. Just knowing Hillcrest existed and that someone had cared for me left me feeling better.

This group home was like a family, but a family of people who understood me.

My next home was a new group home. I lived there with five other kids about the same age as me. We went to school off grounds and we had a caring staff. They actually cooked our dinner, too. The house was cozy and there was always someone to talk to. But most importantly, I didn't have to deal with trying to fit in too much to society or with a family. And I didn't have to deal with ridicule and comments if I couldn't fit in. This group home was like a family, but a family of people who understood me and had been through some of the same things I had. No one laughed at me because I dressed funny. No one laughed or blamed me if I said I had been molested.

But again, the stay was temporary. My agency believed that

kids should live in family settings. My grandmother had passed inspection and I was going to live with her.

Grandma's home was nice, but I missed all the caring adults I had met while in Hillcrest and in my group home. I missed having that many people around who could give me attention or comfort me when I needed it. When I went back to regular school, I got teased for my hair and clothes. Now that I look back, I looked really ragged. No one had ever taught me how to do a better job of dressing myself. But all I thought about was how no one really teased me at Hillcrest or the group home. They accepted me there.

Being in my grandma's home and getting teased at school made my anger and feelings of isolation grow even more. Eventually, I was sent to a residential treatment facility (RTF), where I was supposed to work on anger management.

I really liked it there. It felt like another big group home. We had outings, earned allowance, and every single meal was cooked for us. Activities were set for us, and the best part was having friends and staff who cared. But I did feel like my education suffered a little—there were only two classrooms for all of us, even though we were different ages and grade levels. The teacher was not proficient in all subjects, and we didn't have classes like drama, art, or foreign language.

I stayed at the RTF for approximately nine months. Cindy, my primary staff and role model, was always there for me. She introduced me to journal writing, which I still use today. Unlike some of my family, she noticed my potential and pushed me, but she also helped me work on my weaknesses.

I was so proud when I finished my anger program but I didn't want to leave. We had a goodbye session and all the residents said the nicest things to me. The residents said I was a good friend, they could depend on me, and they thought I did well over the time I was there. I felt good! I still remember those things. Some of the residents and I exchanged addresses.

At my grandma's house I would call some of the residents, and we would write to each other. I still felt very attached to the RTF. At my grandma's house I didn't get what I needed. Of course I got food and shelter, but there wasn't that warmth and caring. There weren't people pushing me to do better, to overcome all I'd been through and to succeed. Don't get me wrong—my grandma cared for me, but she didn't praise me. Also, my sister was around, so I still ran into that heartbreaking ridicule that made me feel so alone.

As the months passed by I grew depressed, and the letters and phone calls slowed. I couldn't keep holding on to the group home. I found other things to do. They weren't necessarily good things, but it kept my mind off my loneliness. Eventually I got pregnant and was moved to a group home with other pregnant teens. Again, I loved it there.

I met people who believed what I had been through.

Most people would say, "Wow. She had her freedom and didn't want it?" It isn't that I didn't want my freedom. It's that I found support, staff members who cared, and other girls who understood me and who had been through just as much as I had. When I had a bad day and was being moody, the staff sometimes understood that there was an underlying issue to it.

That didn't happen at my mother's house or my grandmother's house. When I was in a bad mood at those places, the adult thought I was just being defiant. That made me feel misunderstood and even more alone. The group homes and residential facilities I've been in have really changed my life for the better. For me, a family just meant trying too hard to fit in and be accepted.

The system gave me the chance to experience life in a different way. I didn't have the ridicule, low-self esteem, or shame that I felt at home. I met people who believed what I had been through and didn't hate me for talking about my problems.

There were some problems, of course. It wasn't all good. But overall I think that if I had not been removed from my mother's home and gotten the encouragement and support I needed at group facilities, I wouldn't be where I am today: raising my son, in college, and working part-time.

When people ask for my secret to success, I tell them I used the system to my benefit.

Ja'Nelle later married and worked as a group home counselor.
She is pursuing her degree.

Karolina Zaniesienko

Snow White

By Karol Kwiatkowska

When I got to my first placement in the foster care system, the house looked like it was about to fall apart. The paint on the walls was coming off and you could count like 10 different colors. But inside was scarier. One resident was running around naked. The staff was yelling at her, telling her to put her clothes on. The other residents were screaming too. It seemed like there must be a fire.

Then, when I entered the TV room, they suddenly stopped. Stopped running, stopped screaming. They stopped everything to stare at me, and the expressions on their faces said, "Oh, my God! It's a ghost!"

I was the only white girl in the group home and I was new.

They asked me question after question and I felt like I was in a police station, in one of those interrogation rooms where the cops ask the criminal tons of things, like "What's your name?

Where are you from? What were you doing last night around midnight?"

After a while I got tired of all the questions so I went to my room. I guess the girls didn't like the fact that I left them just like that. Or maybe there was nothing I could've done differently to change the way they started treating me. But from that day on, they started calling me names, like "Snow White," "cracker," and "KKK."

They stopped everything to stare at me. I was the only white girl in the group home.

I felt lonely to begin with. I'd just been separated from my family. I missed my brothers and sisters. Those names made me feel worse. I felt very angry, like I wanted to smack each of the girls. But I couldn't—there were too many of them.

So I read books instead. I didn't like reading back then, but since I had nothing else to do I got used to it. Other times I watched TV or listened to music. I didn't go out because my friends from school were away for the summer. This was the first time I was really on my own. I didn't know what to do with myself, but I knew I had to do something because I couldn't deal with the emptiness.

After a few days, I started talking with some of the staff. I felt awkward at first because I didn't know them, but I tried to start conversations about a movie we had just seen or an article in a newspaper. Soon we were having serious conversations about my problems and theirs. They would give me advice on how to handle the girls who were calling me names, and about my mom who had rejected me when I told her that I was being abused by my stepfather.

Talking to staff helped a lot, but it wasn't enough. I wanted a friend who I could laugh with and make stupid jokes with. I wanted to have fun like a kid again. But to have what I wanted, I had to make the girls in the house who were calling me names like me.

Those girls were wild and funny, but not in a positive way. Liz was the leader of their six-person clique. She was the rudest of the bunch. There were always lines on her forehead and her eyes looked like those of an angry bull.

Then there was Kathy, who was Liz's best friend. Kathy would do anything for Liz. She always made sure that Liz was OK since she was larger in size than Liz, yet she had this baby face that made her look so innocent.

Then there were the four "police officers" who acted and dressed alike. I called them that because they listened to Liz's orders and did what she said. If Liz said, "Go jump in a fire," they would do so with smiles on their faces.

Still, I wanted to be part of that insane clique because I thought it would make me feel like I belonged somewhere. I thought it would help me be less lonely. So for a couple of nights I stayed up thinking, "How am I going to impress those girls?"

Finally, I knew what I had to do. I had to start acting like them. Maybe if I became rude, too, they'd take me in.

For two nights, before I went to bed, I practiced my rudeness. I sat on the bed in front of my pink teddy bear and quietly made up some "smart" lines. Most of them sounded something like, "Shut up, #%$&^%!" Though my lines weren't any good, it felt good to say them. For the next few days I waited for the right moment to use them, and then there it was.

One evening, after dinner, I did my chore as usual, then asked the staff member on duty if I could watch TV. She said no. That was my cue. I exploded and started yelling at the poor woman, who looked like she'd never seen a monster like the one I'd suddenly become. I felt so guilty, but I thought it was my only way into the clique.

The clique noticed my new behavior. They started whispering to each other something like, "You see what she did? What happened to her?" I thought they looked at me with a little more approval from that day on.

Soon the group started asking me for favors like, "Can you get us something from McDonald's?" I figured they were testing me to see if I was down with them, so I did what they asked.

Next, when the group saw me talking to someone who wasn't part of their clique, they'd pump me for information about that person. Sometimes they'd tell me to go to a particular girl and be their "tape recorder." I'd remember what that girl said, then I'd tell them. And the group was nosy! They wanted to know everything about everyone so they could gossip.

One day a new girl named Erika came to the home. Erika had everything that the girls in the group wanted but didn't have—a good job as a salesperson, a very attractive boyfriend, even a car. She was also pretty and intelligent. The group couldn't stand it. They wanted me to act like Erika's friend, while really spying on her.

Slowly, Erika and I started to build our friendship. We would go shopping, to a movie, or just hang out around the group home talking and laughing. It was like we were best friends, except for one thing. I was repeating all our conversations to the group.

I hated myself for being such a fake friend. But I felt even worse when Erika found out what I was doing. Liz told her. Erika looked so deeply sad. *I was lonely again, but at least I was being my real self.* That's when I realized how stupid I'd been: Erika could have been the friend I really needed. Instead, I'd betrayed her to be friends with the girls in the group.

I wanted to apologize, but I was too scared to talk to Erika. "I am such a cruel beast," I thought. After a while I just wanted to disappear. Erika never spoke to me again. After that, the group accepted me. Still, I missed Erika.

I tried to push my guilty feelings out of the way. And I really did have fun with that group for a while. But I also saw many people hurt because we would pretend to be their friends, then laugh at them. Usually we were laughing not because we thought they were worse than us, but because we thought they were better than us. Being mean and putting people down helped us feel better about ourselves. But soon it was me that everyone betrayed.

One night we decided to play "hide and seek" with the staff. I hid under my bed. After a while the staff announced that if I didn't come out they'd put me on phone restriction.

I wanted to show them how tough I was, so I stayed under the bed. Then the staff threatened to put me on TV restriction. I gave up. I mean, this was TV.

When I came out, I found out that I was the only one playing the game. The girls started laughing at me. I felt worse than when I first stepped into that house.

Since I saw that my people weren't really my people, I requested a staff-resident meeting. I wanted to talk about my behavior. The meeting started with Ms. White saying to me, "You were such a good girl when you came here. What happened?"

I turned red and during the rest of the meeting I apologized to everybody (except Erika, who had moved out). I also explained why I'd been doing so badly. I promised them that I wouldn't disappoint them again.

Somehow they understood me and forgave me. The meeting ended with all of us laughing and making jokes. I still felt awkward, but I was happy to step back and be me again, the "goodie girl."

The girls in the group stopped talking to me. Then they went back to calling me names, and I went back to reading and watching TV. I was lonely again, but at least I was being my real self.

Finally the staff moved me for safety reasons—the group was trying to get violent with me. I was relieved to go to a new group home. It was a chance to start over. And there was no doubt in my mind how I would handle myself. In my new home, I would form friendships slowly and not change for anyone. I said to myself, "I'm just going to be the person that I am, and if someone doesn't like that, then too bad."

I've been in my group home for one and a half years now, and so far my plan has been a success. The girls in this home are older and more mature than those in my last home, so they don't have as much to prove. And I feel accepted for me.

I do still get lonely from time to time. Living apart from your family and your longtime friends is a difficult situation no matter who you are. But I always remind myself that it's even lonelier to pretend to be someone you're not.

Karol was 18 when she wrote this story.

Marcus Pierno

Overcoming My
Fear of Gays

By Sharif Berkeley

I recently moved to a foster care group home in Manhattan. I was looking forward to it, but then I began to have second thoughts because the facility had as many gays as straight people. This was a problem because for the longest time I've been one of those people who teases and slanders gay people.

In the past I hadn't had many run-ins with the people I called "faggots," besides seeing them on the train at night or on TV. To me, they were misfits of society who had serious mental disorders. I was raised to be manly. I was taught that men were supposed to like women, not other men, and that gays were one of the reasons why the world was going to hell.

I've been in various group homes where the residents were all straight. All the guys were always very self-conscious about the way we acted towards one another. We didn't touch each other too affectionately. We not only made fun of gays constantly, but also of the residents who stayed in the bathroom too long (we used to say they were bustin' nuts). It was all part of being a guy. You had to walk like a guy, talk about girls who have big body parts, and make fun of "faggots."

But now, in my new group home, the tables were turned on me because I had to live right in the middle of the people I made fun of. I thought all the gays would want to touch me (and do other kinds of things to me that aren't fit to print in this article).

On my first day there, I was given a personal tour of the group home. The staff showed me the dining room, lobby, and such. Then they took me to the upper floors where the residents lived and showed me their rooms. (This was the eye-opening part.) As we roamed through the rooms of the residents, who were not home at the time, I was awestruck by pictures of musclebound men and male models lining the walls. I thought to myself, "If this isn't sick, I don't know what is."

Later on I actually saw a group of gay residents. Some stopped what they were doing and gave me this, "Is this the new addition to our group?" look. It made me a bit nervous, so I moved on about my business.

The concept of someone being gay was inconceivable to me. It was like putting two and two together and getting five.

During my first week I kept thinking, "If any of these fags touches me or even looks at me, I'll beat them straight." Beyond that, my attitude towards the whole situation was, keep to myself, speak only to the straight residents, and stay out of the house by keeping myself busy with work.

I was intimidated because I felt that if I did the slightest thing, like brush up against them or even look at them, they would think that I was gay, too. I stopped doing impressions of gay people. A few of them started to say that I was gay because I kept to myself.

The concept of someone being gay was inconceivable to me. It was like putting two and two together and getting five. Some of them acted as if they were women with wigs on, and some would run after each other screaming. I would also overhear some of them referring to each other as "she," then talking about themselves like girls do in school.

Just when I thought I had seen it all, I saw a gay resident with permed hair, hazel contacts, and a denim skirt with a pink spandex tank top. Events such as these were as common as milk on cereal. Every day seemed to be more weird than the last. And to top it off, even the new manager I had at work turned out to be gay. I felt surrounded, like a thief in a botched-up bank robbery.

Time after time I thought to myself, "If I could move out of here I would." But I didn't want to move back in with my family because the problems of my past would happen all over again, and I didn't have enough money to get out on my own. So as it turned out, I was stuck. There was nothing I could do but live there for the time being.

I didn't think that I could ever come to terms with my prejudice (or "phobia," as one might call it). But eventually there was a slight turn of events which made me put aside the immature feelings I had about gays.

Each day at noon everyone came down for lunch. There were about five sets of tables in the dining area. Most of the time I either sat by myself or with people who I knew were straight.

One day, as I sat at the table eating, a straight friend came and sat down with me. He didn't have any problems with the gay population and often spoke with them without uneasiness. He lived in the facility way before I got there and had gotten to know them well, even though he admits he felt the same way I did when he first moved in.

As we sat and talked a while, one of the gay residents came and sat down with us because he wanted to speak with my friend. Of course I had nothing to say to that particular person, but the conversation went on. They were talking about a movie they just saw, one I had also seen, so it sparked my attention. I noticed that a lot of what was said and the different topics that were brought up didn't have anything to do with being gay. (I thought that all "they" wanted to talk about were their boyfriends and a construction worker guy on some TV commercial.)

I then started to put my two cents into the conversation. Then another gay resident happened to overhear what we

As I got to know the gay residents, I realized they are decent people just like anyone.

were discussing and came and sat down with us. During the conversation I noticed that I had a lot of things in common with them. We spoke about movies we had seen, stupid things that people did which made us laugh, clothes, and places we liked to go. To my surprise I actually enjoyed the conversation, and I even got a chance to throw in my sense of humor. I got to know a couple of the gay residents and felt a little more at ease being among them.

As the days went on I got to know all of the gay residents, and it made me realize that they are decent people just like anyone. They respected my being heterosexual and didn't make comments about my lifestyle or try to influence me.

It took two months, but I've learned to accept who they are and that they can't be changed. The concept of being gay is still something that I don't completely understand and probably never will, but all things in the world are not meant to be understood.

I'm not saying that everything is peachy now, but I have to live among the gay population and I can't see myself hiding and secluding myself. I have to watch how I joke around because I'm still a little self-conscious.

Being prejudiced against people who have done nothing to you is one of the most immature things in the world. I consider myself to be a very mature person, and being prejudiced against gay people was a perfect display of how I could act my shoe size and not my age.

Sharif was 16 when he wrote this story. He attended Lehman College and worked in information technology.

Jamaal Pascall

Fight for Your Respect

By Anonymous

Being in a group home can be like living in a palace (but not in the comfy sense). You have the King or Queen of the Hill, you have the Followers, and you have the Fool.

When you're the King or Queen, oh yeah, life is grand. People give you props and they don't mess with you. You ask them to do things for you and they do it. Ah, to be the King or Queen. (How do y'all do it?)

When you're a Follower, you're probably not so happy. But if you agree with what the King and Queen say (even when half the time you don't know what the bleep they're talking about), then you get considerable props.

But when you're the Fool (sigh), life can be full of thorns. Everyone's dissing you, laughing at you, embarrassing you. Oh, you're in the spotlight, alright. You star as the butt of everyone's jokes.

Still, in my opinion, to be the group home Fool or "scapegoat" isn't so bad. Before y'all start thinking that I need help (which I do, but that's beside the point!), I'll say this: At least the scapegoat has enough respect and self-worth not to be a Follower.

I want to talk about a girl who was a scapegoat in my group home and who I now consider one of my very good friends. Her name is Violet.

I remember the day Violet moved into my group home in Queens, New York. We had been in a previous placement together, and when we saw each other we hugged and reminisced about the kids we knew in our old group home. Violet and I didn't talk that much back then, but she was cool.

Her first day in the new group home was alright. But after a week, the guys started dissing her. See, she was what I would call, in the nicest way possible, a child at heart. And as the days went by and the kids noticed that Violet talked funny and acted a little too childish, the boys gave her hell. They dissed the way she talked and the way she dressed. They pushed her, hit her, or threw things at her. The girls either bullied her, took advantage of her, or just laughed at her.

When you're the Fool (sigh), life can be full of thorns.

I wasn't much of a good friend to Violet because I was laughing at all their jokes, and sometimes even I would make fun of how she talked. Eventually, I started to feel guilty. One day, when one of the girls threw a pool ball at Violet, that's when I decided to try my best not to laugh at her or dis her. Violet was a good person. She was nice to everyone. Why should she get this kind of treatment?

See, I had to remember this: I was the scapegoat a long time ago. Back in junior high school, all them junior playa wannabees would make fun of me. Oh boy. I was the centerfool of attention.

They used to play a game "in honor" of me called "germs."

The object of the game was that if I touched you, you had to tag someone else so that you wouldn't have "germs." The only way that you'd be safe from the germs was if your fingers were crossed. Otherwise, you'd get them.

Can you imagine how I felt at that time? I wanted to disappear and die. And I was the Queen of the Scapegoats for a good six years. That's how I know firsthand how scapegoats feel. I didn't stand up for myself until 7th grade. That's when I decided I had enough and went to confront the boy who started the cooties game.

I said to him, "Look, this stuff has gone too far! Third and 4th were okay. But 7th grade? C'mon! This is wack. Can't you leave me alone and grow up?"

Ha! As if I could reason with a 13-year-old still acting like a 9-year-old. I don't remember what he said after that, but I do remember that we fought. He gave me some bruises, but I gave him some bruises back and a busted lip.

After my fight, I paid a bad price. About five or six guys ganged up on me. After I was dealt with, I was angry because I felt more embarrassed than hurt. But when June came around, they didn't bother me too much. I guess they decided to pay more attention to their schoolwork since they were failing two or three classes.

But back to Violet. Like I was saying, after the incident when the girl threw a pool ball at her, I kinda woke up. It just wasn't fair for me to treat Violet like I didn't know her just 'cause she was a scapegoat. I decided to be a friend to her. But it was a little bit hard because I couldn't help laughing at the jokes that the other kids were saying about her.

One day, Desi (my ex-friend) and I were talking and Violet was passing by. Desi told Violet that I was dissing her. I shook my head and said, "No, I didn't," but Violet wouldn't believe me. Plus, I was laughing so hard because Desi made me laugh.

Next thing you know, Violet and I were arguing and Desi was

laughing her head off and enjoying herself. Violet called me a curse. After Violet and I stopped arguing and Violet went to her room, it occurred to me that Desi started this whole charade. So because of that, I stopped hanging out with Desi.

I wrote a short and simple letter to Violet, advising her not to be nice to jerks. We didn't talk for a few weeks. But at the Christmas party, we made up. She gave me an apology letter and a stuffed Koala bear and I gave her a card and a small statue. (Awwww....) After Christmas, the kids didn't bother her as much as before. Violet had learned how to stand up for herself. The kids still wouldn't hang out with her, but we stayed friends.

I know firsthand how scapegoats feel. I didn't stand up for myself until 7th grade.

And to prove that scapegoats can be successful, Violet was moved to one of those Independent Living apartments. I think she's still there (until she turns 21, of course). I wish her lots of luck and success.

What I have to say to all of you group home scapegoats is this:

1) Don't kiss up! If you're trying to be a friend to someone and he/she treats you like crap, stay away from them. It just doesn't pay! If you continue to be nice to those types of people, they'll use you like a basketball. Respect them and their space, but don't kiss up. Violet tried to be friends with everyone, but all she got was a kick in the butt because they didn't accept her for who she was.

Whoever in your group home plays the Queen is no better than you. Trust. I don't care if they were in a gang, in jail, a juvenile penitentiary, cuckoo house, or if they have 500 men or $500 worth of Tommygear. You deserve to get respect! You've been through enough and you don't need any more problems. Only be nice to those who are nice and friendly to you.

2) If a posse pushes you around or plays hot potato with your stuff, stand up for yourself. If it continues, I'm sorry, but the first

thing you should do is (gulp) tell staff. If that doesn't work, tell the group home supervisor or the director. And if that doesn't work, well then, uh...do what you think you gotta do.

3) Always remember, sometimes the King or Queen can be dethroned and he/she may become the Fool. I think eventually the others will respect and admire you for standing up for yourself. Who knows? You may be crowned the new "Queen!"

But don't think of yourself as the King, Queen, Jack, Ace, Follower, or the Fool (scapegoat). Think of yourself as YOU and bring out your good qualities. Build your own throne and rule your own castle, happily but wisely.

(And now, if y'all excuse me, I think someone's playing hot potato with my bra....)

The writer was 19 when she wrote this story.

Rafael Manashirov

Jasmine, the Scapegoat

By Angela R.

"That's why your mother abandoned you in McDonald's with a Happy Meal, you stupid fool."

"At least I have a mother."

"Who's your father, Ronald McDonald?"

These are a few of the insults that are thrown into Jasmine's face almost every day in our group home, but that's not where it ends.

I've been in the same placements with Jasmine for over a year and I've come to realize that everybody takes their anger out on her. One girl will get into an argument with Jasmine, then that girl's friends will make it into a bigger argument. Most of the time she ends up getting jumped.

One time they trashed Jasmine's room after she got into a fight with them. They ripped down her posters and pulled the head off her stuffed animal. They threw her clothes into a pile and pissed on them, and then they peed on her bed.

From that time on, I felt sorry for Jasmine.

I have to admit that I haven't always treated Jasmine much better. Many times I've taken my anger out on her. I was quick to argue with Jasmine because I knew the rest of the girls would be on my side. It made me feel superior to her. Sometimes I was glad to see her get picked on, as long as it wasn't me who they were dissing.

> *I was quick to argue with Jasmine because I knew the rest of the girls would be on my side.*

I stopped teasing her after I realized why I was doing it. When I was living back home, I got verbally trashed by my father all the time. He would call me "white trash" and "fat and lazy."

I realized that many kids who've been verbally abused or neglected by family members will take out their anger on weaker kids. It's a vicious cycle that needs to be stopped.

But other girls in my group home don't seem to realize why they do it or make up excuses. It's easy for them to pick on Jasmine because everyone is already against her.

Most of the girls say that Jasmine starts it off by getting an attitude with them. I always point out that her attitude is a result of all the abuse she takes.

"Why should she be nice all of a sudden?" I ask the girls. "She knows that in the next five minutes you'll be getting your nasty attitude with her."

Jasmine was much weaker and quicker to have a breakdown in our previous placement. She's much stronger now because of all of the stuff she's been through. She's learned how to stick up for herself.

But because she had a weak personality before, people are used to taking advantage of her. Even the new girls talk down to Jasmine because they know they can get away with it.

Most scapegoats have been abused all their lives and don't know how to stop it. A lot of times I actually see Jasmine feeding into it. If people aren't dissing her or arguing with her, then they're not talking to her at all. So she'll do things to start arguments. Maybe scapegoats like the negative attention. Maybe the negative attention is better than no attention at all.

I realized that many kids who were abused at home will take out their anger on weaker kids.

The abuse Jasmine takes won't end soon. Maybe she won't get into any more fights, but she'll still be the one excluded from conversations. Girls will still dis her and make her feel unwanted, but I plan to be on her side.

Angela was 16 when she wrote this story.

Isadora Versiani

Girls Like Me

By Rana Sino

When I tell people I live in a group home, they automatically assume that I'm absolutely miserable. But the truth is, I'm not.

Now don't get me wrong, there's plenty to stress me out. I live with 11 other girls, and two different staff every couple of hours. I never knew how aggravating so many girls under one roof could be.

First of all, every other week, some girl has her period, and we all have to deal with her mood swings and attitude. When a girl who normally comes home talkative and funny, and instead curses, holds her stomach, and moans, "Leave me the hell alone" or "I hate being a girl," it means only one thing.

Then there are the females in my group home who like to "borrow" things from the other girls, and then "forget" they have whatever it is they "borrowed." I don't always lock my door and sometimes the girls make themselves at home in my room. The girls take things like nail polish, polish remover, clippers, nail filers, makeup, combs, my hairbrush, perfume, tweezers, shaving cream, razors, shampoo, conditioner, and sometimes even my clothes. When I notice that something is missing (and I always do), I end up having to do my own search of their rooms.

As much as the girls aggravate me sometimes, I try to love them all like sisters, but some of them don't feel the same way about each other. Some of them feel that the only way to solve a problem is to "duke it out."

Like one time two roommates fought about a pair of pantyhose. It went from the question, "Where'd you get those?" to a fight that was so big the staff wasn't able to hold those girls apart.

Now, as far as staff goes, there are some staff who I get along with and some staff who at least don't bother me, but then there are the staff who none of the girls like.

Two staff in particular are always trying to make us feel that we are lucky to be living in the house. Then they talk behind our backs about how much they want us to get out. Those are the staff who make up whatever rules they want for the house and then say that they are going "by the book." Those are also the staff who want to limit everything we get, including food, money, and visitors.

When I tell people I live in a group home, they automatically assume that I'm miserable.

I'm only allowed two regular visitors, my brother and my boyfriend. But even with them, those staff members give me a hard time. I mean, I understand why they won't let me invite my boyfriend in my room, but I think that my brother should be able to come to my house whenever he wants, go anywhere in the house he wants, including my room or the kitchen to pour himself a drink, or even downstairs to watch TV, as long as he stays out of trouble. But some staff are always saying he can't do this or he can't do that.

These are the same staff who, if we're five minutes late for meals, say we can't eat. They also say we can only get a single portion of food. If we want more, all we get from them is, "McDonald's is right around the corner." The other day, I asked one of the staff if I could boil two hot dogs to take to work, and you know what he said to me? "Sorry, it's against state policy to cook food in the house and take it to work or school."

I thought, "Are you kidding me? I just want to boil two frickin' hot dogs!"

So yes, I could complain on and on about life in this group home. But the truth is, the biggest part of me is happy to be where I am. I consider the girls my sisters, not only because we all live in the same house, but also because we share similar problems.

Some of the staff are like aunts, and I have a new father figure, Mr. Cordova. He is my primary. (A primary is a staff member assigned to one or two girls, whose job it is to act as the parent to those girls when it comes to school, work, and any other personal matters.)

Mr. Cordova taught me not to hate everybody just because of the way my father treated me. He made me feel comfortable talking to him about whatever is going through my head, and he always tries to help. He shows all the girls attention and love—even the girls who are not his primaries call him "dad." But mostly he showers attention on me, because I'm his primary. He's really something.

All that goes a long way to explaining why, with all the hassles I face every day, I haven't left yet. Part of it's because I want to take advantage of the system for college, my medical needs, and all my other living needs. But more than that, it's because I actually like the place.

When I used to live with my father, I felt as if I was living in hell. He cursed me and hit me and always said nasty things to me. My dad never gave me any freedom. I practically had to live in his grocery store just so I wouldn't be out of his sight.

Now I have the freedom that I dreamed of when I was stuck in that store with my father. If I were still with my father, I would not be going to the awesome school I'm going to and I seriously doubt I would be a senior and on my way to college.

I consider the girls my sisters because we share similar problems.

If I were still living with that man, I would not have the confidence in myself that I now have. I would not have the freedom to meet cool new people. And it would be hard to have my boyfriend, who at one point, my father wanted to kill.

I remember the first time I went out, right after I'd moved into the group home. I had just gotten off of house restriction, and the next day was my 18th birthday. I spent the whole day with one of my really good friends.

The next day, I went to a concert with friends to celebrate my birthday. When I got home, it was 1:30 in the morning. But when I walked in the house, I saw the girls who I'd only known for a week in the dining room screaming, "SURPRISE!"

I thought to myself, "Wow, this is my new home."

Rana was 20 when she wrote this story.

Edward Cortez

Five Steps Behind

By Kareem Banks

Coming into the system at age 10, people told me all kinds of stuff about the bullies, the thieves, and the lack of freedom. All this was true. Living in a boys' group home was like living in a scared straight program. What nobody warned me about, though, was how unprepared I'd be to face life on my own after living in one of those homes for seven years.

I was nervous when I came into the group home, but I hoped it would teach me to be responsible in a grown-up kind of way and change me into a better person.

The group home rewarded us with snacks and later bedtimes when we showed we could handle chores like vacuuming, washing dishes, and cleaning the bathroom without being asked. I was angry about having my freedom taken away, but after a while I felt I was becoming more mature. All the bad things people told me about group homes made me want to do what I had to do so I could get out quicker.

A few months later, though, all the staff who really cared for us left or found better jobs. The new staff wasn't experienced with adolescents and had an "I don't give a damn about these kids, just give me my paycheck" attitude. Since our parents weren't around, I felt it was their job to be our parents. Their jobs are not like working a register—if you're not built for the challenge or don't care for us, then don't waste our time.

But they stayed, making my life hard. If I asked their advice, they would always tell me to talk to my social worker, who came in only three days a week and always missed meetings with me. If I was depressed about something, like a home visit being cancelled or a visit that went bad, they wouldn't sit down and talk to me to find out what was wrong or if I was all right. It was like having blind or deaf babysitters.

No one ever talked to me about going to college or vocational school, how to have a career, how to rent and keep an apartment, how to resolve conflicts with people, or even how to cook a hamburger all the way through.

No one ever talked to me about going to college, or even how to cook a hamburger.

Cooking should have been easy to teach since the staff cooked every day. But when I asked to be taught they'd say, "Y'all know we don't allow y'all thieving asses to be in this kitchen." They didn't want us in the kitchen because most of the residents would steal food from the pantry. The only thing that I know how to cook today is fried fish, grilled cheese sandwiches, and those little packs of soup.

Let's talk about the group home school. They would teach us way below regular standards. In 10th grade math class I was assigned fractions that I learned in the 7th grade.

One day I came home on a visit and saw my 12-year-old brother doing his homework at the living room table. "What kind of work you doing?" I asked him.

"Math," he said. He handed me his worksheet. It was poly-nomials (part of algebra), which was the same exact thing I was getting in 10th grade at the group home.

Worse, he was doing it with no problem. It was easy for him! I had a hard time finding a formula for a bunch of letters and numbers. I really got upset thinking what my life would be like when I left the group home.

When I eventually got discharged, I desperately needed a job. I didn't know what was needed for a job interview besides a tie, slacks, and a dress shirt. I went on three job inter-views and was turned away each time because I didn't have something that I didn't know I needed.

First, it was a state ID that I didn't have. I got one. The second time it was a Social Security card I didn't have. I got that. The third time I was turned down because I didn't bring my birth certificate. I got that, too—but I felt five steps behind, not know-ing something that everyone else seemed to know.

This is how I've had to learn—by rejection and making mis-takes. I feel we should be taught what to expect ahead of time. I want to be prepared for what's coming up so I don't have to ask for help.

If I were in charge of a group home, I would try to make liv-ing there more like real life. I'd try to make sure every discharged resident is properly prepared for society instead of feeling left behind and not ready.

The group home would teach things residents need to know to be independent after leaving care—how to manage money, make a budget, and keep a job. Young people would be taught how to cook, clean, get along with people, and pay bills. I would try to get people who could offer job opportunities involved with the agency so residents would have jobs to go to after they leave.

When a resident gets discharged, he would be able to keep in touch and visit the group home to learn more skills to deal with obstacles he faces. I would only hire qualified staff who love kids. That way, residents who feel stressed, angry, or lonely would have staff who are willing to listen, be supportive, and help them through the hardship of being away from their families.

If I were in charge of a group home, I would try to make living there more like real life.

I feel it's the system's responsibility to hire good staff. Every two or three months, I'd have residents rate the staff so that everyone knows which staff members are good for the kids and the agency.

The staff who the residents rate highest would receive pay raises to reduce the chance of them leaving to find better-paying jobs. That way, the good staff will get good pay and the residents will be better prepared for society when they leave.

Kareem was 21 when he wrote this story.
He later joined the U.S. Navy.

Emilia Martinez

Man With a Plan

By Michael Orr

I'd been living at my residential treatment center (RTC) about a month, having fun and not worrying about anything, when I met Earl. He was one of the resident troublemakers, in and out of jail all the time.

When the staff workers introduced him to me, he stuck his hand out to give me a pound and said, "What's good?" I gave him a pound and told him I was chilling out and relaxing. Then as I went walking toward the living room, he turned me around and sucker punched me out of nowhere. We were fighting for at least 10 minutes before staff broke us up. I had a busted upper lip from this dude and I didn't even know why he wanted to fight.

Earl was a Crip, the only one on campus. He was outnumbered one to two or three dozen, but that didn't stop him from representing his colors. Earl kept on causing trouble with everybody until he turned 21. In New York, that's when you "age out" and have to leave foster care and live on your own. Earl had no family, no friends, and no place to go or live. We all witnessed that day when staff handed him some plastic bags and subway fare, wished him a happy birthday (talk about adding insult to injury), and sent him with his belongings to a shelter.

I didn't feel bad for him at all because he brought it on himself. The thing that got me was how they sent him on his way. I was really upset about their actions because I pictured myself in Earl's shoes for that moment. I knew the administration workers were grimy, but what they did to that fool was messed up.

Maybe they had this planned just for him. Or maybe it applied to anyone who had no place to go. All I knew was I wasn't going to let it happen to me.

When I first got put in foster care at 13, I thought I wasn't going to be there long and I wanted to go back with my family. Then I started noticing kids getting discharged to their families and ending up back in foster care a month or two later. I decided then to make the best of foster care. Years later, seeing what happened to Earl made me determined not to become another trapped statistic of the system.

I had a job on campus in the cafeteria. It only paid $25 a week, but I began to put every cent I earned away and started thinking about living on my own. I knew the sooner I started, the better it would be for me.

I was 17 years old when they kicked Earl out. I was going to be 18 in three months so I felt I would be their next target. I had to get on my grind ASAP.

My social worker tried to convince me to go to a group home every time he had a chance, but I refused. I wanted to go straight to an Independent Living (IL) house, not a group home. (IL is a program that teaches teens who are aging out of foster care how to live on their own.)

At the RTC, there were people smoking, drinking, male staff

having sex with female residents, people stealing from each other and lots of fights. I had no privacy. In IL I would be one step closer to being on my own. To qualify, I'd have to have a job or be going to college or vocational school.

One of my school advisers introduced me to a program called VESID, which helps teens and adults find work or pays for them to go to school. I didn't know what field I'd be interested in, but since I had worked in the cafeteria my school advisor suggested I study culinary arts. I decided to give it a shot.

I had to complete the course in three months to get my certificate. But after two and a half months I quit to play my final year on the varsity basketball team. Basketball was one of the few things that kept me motivated and I loved playing.

Then, during the course of my basketball season, my social worker assigned me to go to a group home, without telling me. That was a messed up surprise for me. I knew I needed to leave the RTC. I was getting older and it seemed like everyone else was getting younger. But I wanted to leave the way I planned with my workers from my agency. I'd lived at the RTC for almost five years, and it was a shock to have to leave everything all at once.

I was angry they had made a decision behind my back. I started thinking, "What was the point of having all those meetings if what I said was not going to make a difference?"

A few days after I moved, I had another meeting with staff. When we discussed my future, I put on my serious face and told them my plan to go to independent living and how good I had done on the campus. I even told them about what my social worker did and demanded they not pull that same stunt on me. They said I would be informed about any news that comes up about my future.

On my 19th birthday I played my final game on the varsity team. Now I was ready to focus on getting a job and getting out of the group home. I prepared to find work at any place that was hiring.

I filled out applications at some stores but had no luck. My friend Jayvonne told me K-Mart was hiring, so I filled out an application. One week later, I went to an orientation and was handed a folder with my schedule inside. I walked back to the group home feeling surprised and proud of myself for getting a job.

About three months later, after my next meeting, I signed up for Section 8 (a program that gives you vouchers to help pay your rent) and a savings account. I had a job and stayed out of trouble. I completed all of the tasks they asked me to do with no problem, so there was no way they could deny me a spot on the IL list.

After six months, I was finally able to move to IL housing. When I received the news, I went nuts. I felt so great about it I started packing up my things immediately. The next day a van came to take me and my stuff to my new placement.

The only problem was that the new placement was right by campus, and I was afraid I'd be around the same people all the time. Sure enough, I arrived at the house to find lots of people from the campus hanging out. My new roommate had invited them to chill there and do whatever they wanted. They were drinking, smoking, and sleeping on blankets like it was a shelter.

Seeing what happened to Earl made me determined not to become another trapped statistic of the system.

There was never any privacy and it was always noisy at the house, so I dealt with it by spending most of my time at the b-ball court. A month or so later, I was moved to another IL house. I got my Section 8 vouchers and started searching for an apartment. I went to a real estate broker to help me find a place to live quickly before I left care.

He found a place that he wanted me to see, but when I got there the super had the wrong set of keys. I was tired and frustrated so I decided to stick with the place without seeing it. I signed a two-year lease, put down the first month's rent and security deposit and got the keys. When I went back to the apartment I was surprised to see how good it looked. I couldn't wait to move in.

My 21st birthday finally arrived and it was a breath of fresh air for me. I went to the IL office to get my grant money and the last of the money I was getting from the IL program. Then I celebrated my birthday and my accomplishment with my girlfriend Erica.

When we discussed my future, I put on my serious face and told them my plan.

Now I've been living at my apartment for almost a year with Erica and things are going fine. I do some part-time work and I get to see my family more. I feel a lot better about myself, and I feel that Erica and I are changing for the better. I have grown into a mature young adult and I try to show my younger peers what they need to do after they get out of foster care.

At times I catch myself thinking about the decisions I made to get me to this point. If I had an opportunity to do it differently, I wouldn't change anything. To me the greatest thing about going from foster care to having my own place was the journey itself.

Michael was 21 when he wrote this story. He later married Erica, had two children, and worked as a security guard.

Ora Obhas

Missing My Old Group Home

By Max Moran

I never thought I would say this in a million years, but sometimes I do miss my old group home. It's been six months since I left, yet it seems like yesterday. Even though there were more negatives than positives during my four and a half years living there, I still remember all the people who helped me stay on the right path.

I remember one resident who had already given up on life. He never went to school. All he did was smoke weed all day long. But I think in me he saw himself. At that time I was working and going to school, and deep inside he knew he could do it, too. But he was just too lazy to sacrifice and commit himself to something positive. He used to tell me that if anyone was going to get out from the group home and make it in life, it was me.

It was so sad seeing somebody so young and yet so old. To

me, the biggest injustice in life is having a dream, yet not having the chance to make it into a reality.

To be honest with you, most group home kids are not that bad. Sometimes all we need is for somebody to guide us, to show us that he or she cares. Someone to yell at us when we're messing up and to calm us down when life in a group home stresses us out.

It seemed that I always had something to complain about. If it wasn't the food, it was the allowance. I simply hated living in a place where the food was locked up as if it was gold. I hated living in a place where everyone had to suffer when one resident did something bad. When there was a fight, the TV and the phone were always shut off.

I never used the group home as an excuse to fail.

That was when I used to go up to my room with my pen and pad to get poetic. I usually wrote about my world. A place that was so much more beautiful than the one I was experiencing. In my world I was more than a name on a piece of paper, and I never felt lonely or depressed.

In my fantasy world my parents would get me a brand new car as a high school graduation present, and Janet Jackson was my girlfriend. But that's a fantasy for another day.

Other times when I got depressed, I used to go to the church next door to the group home where there was a basketball court. Soon residents and neighborhood kids would join in.

It's funny how a simple game helped me deal with my depression and loneliness. More often than not I was the shortest player on the court, but I never saw anybody play harder than me. My jumpshot had to be perfect. I wasn't satisfied unless the ball went right through the net.

I got out all my anger on the court. I wanted every rebound to be mine. Every assist had to belong to me, and if my team was losing it was up to me to make a comeback. Even if we were losing 20 to nothing, I was still playing hard. People thought I was crazy, but giving up has never been in my vocabulary.

Life was so simple then. If a girl dumped me or if I got into some stupid argument with another resident, if someone stole something from my room or if I got put on restriction, all I had to do was play ball and all my problems went away. At least for a couple of hours.

I really miss those days so bad! Father Time is so unfair; he only goes forward. I miss the times we went on trips and the girls from other group homes came along. We used to act as if we had never seen a female before. I was always the shy one, so all I could do was sit back and admire their beauty. So many cuties! Sweet as honey! Yet they had some of the same problems I did and they weren't shy about expressing them.

It's never too early to open up your eyes and realize that the day will arrive when you will no longer be allowed in the group home.

I think that it's never too early to open up your eyes and realize that the day will arrive when you will no longer be allowed in the group home. The time will come when you will have to face the real world, so plan your future now before it's too late. Finish high school and, if you already have, then go on to college. Don't limit yourself. Life is a struggle, we can all agree on that. Yet you must be strong, for only the strong survive.

Living in a group home has made me strong and today I'm not afraid of anything. I never used the group home as an excuse to fail and you shouldn't either, because deep inside of us lies a warrior that should never give up. Who cares what your peers may say? Don't feel like an outcast because you live in foster care. Instead, use it to your advantage.

Today I'm 20 years old, I go to college, and share an apartment with someone. There are a lot more people like me and we're all living proof that if you persevere, good things will happen to you. I'm not afraid of my destiny because I'm choosing it.

My life has changed for the better, yet sometimes I get sad thinking about why my parents were so cruel to me. But then I remember that I grew into a decent human being without them, so I guess somebody else was looking out for me.

When I lived in the group home, every time I came home there was always someone to greet me. Either in a good way or bad way. Today when I come home, all I do is check my messages. My life is much better now in a lot of ways, yet I can't forget the times we used to stay up all night in the group home talking about our futures. Talking about who the real mack of the house was.

Today I live next to an elementary school, and sometimes when I'm alone I can hear the laughter of little kids. Then I wonder how my childhood would have been if I had parents. Sometimes I would do anything to be 10 years younger. When I was 10, all I worried about was playing ball and hanging out with my friends.

Back then I was too innocent to worry about my physical appearance, too young to notice the opposite sex. Back in the days I'd rather have a quarter to play video games than a kiss from a beautiful girl. It's a shame that my childhood was so short, yet it's hard to forget something that was so pure.

Then reality sets in and I find myself alone. Alone in my own room, trying to break free from these imaginary chains.

When sadness settles inside of me, I wish I could go and play one last game with the fellas.

Damn you father! Damn you for leaving me when I was 2. Damn you, mother! You weren't much better than he was.

At times like these, when sadness settles inside of me, I wish I could go back to my old group home, grab a basketball, and play one last game with the fellas. But I'm so far away, in distance and in time.

Maybe I should go to the basketball court across the street and try to make new memories. Yet I would only be fooling myself, because it wouldn't be the same without the fellas.

I love you, Taylor Street group home, even though you made me into a man before my time.

Max was 20 when he wrote this story. He graduated from college and social work school and became a therapist.

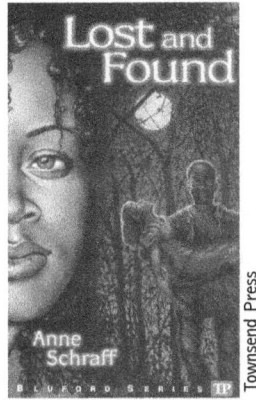

Lost and Found

Darcy Wills winced at the loud rap music coming from her sister's room.

My rhymes were rockin'
MC's were droppin'
People shoutin' and hip-hoppin'
Step to me and you'll be inferior
'Cause I'm your lyrical superior.

Darcy went to Grandma's room. The darkened room smelled of lilac perfume, Grandma's favorite, but since her stroke Grandma did not notice it, or much of anything.

"Bye, Grandma," Darcy whispered from the doorway. "I'm going to school now."

Just then, the music from Jamee's room cut off, and Jamee rushed into the hallway.

The teen characters in the Bluford novels, a fiction series by Townsend Press, struggle with many of the same difficult issues that our students write about. Here's the first chapter from *Lost and Found*, by Anne Schraff, the first book in the series. In this novel, high school sophomore Darcy contends with the return of her long-absent father, the troubling behavior of her younger sister Jamee, and the beginning of her first relationship.

"Like she even hears you," Jamee said as she passed Darcy. Just two years younger than Darcy, Jamee was in eighth grade, though she looked older.

"It's still nice to talk to her. Sometimes she understands. You want to pretend she's not here or something?"

"She's not," Jamee said, grabbing her backpack.

"Did you study for your math test?" Darcy asked. Mom was an emergency room nurse who worked rotating shifts. Most of the time, Mom was too tired to pay much attention to the girls' schoolwork. So Darcy tried to keep track of Jamee.

"Mind your own business," Jamee snapped.

"You got two D's on your last report card," Darcy scolded. "You wanna flunk?" Darcy did not want to sound like a nagging parent, but Jamee wasn't doing her best. Maybe she couldn't make A's like Darcy, but she could do better.

Jamee stomped out of the apartment, slamming the door behind her. "Mom's trying to get some rest!" Darcy yelled. "Do you have to be so selfish?" But Jamee was already gone, and the apartment was suddenly quiet.

Darcy loved her sister. Once, they had been good friends. But now all Jamee cared about was her new group of rowdy friends. They leaned on cars outside of school and turned up rap music on their boom boxes until the street seemed to tremble like an earthquake. Jamee had even stopped hanging out with her old friend Alisha Wrobel, something she used to do every weekend.

Darcy went back into the living room, where her mother sat in the recliner sipping coffee. "I'll be home at 2:30, Mom," Darcy said. Mom smiled faintly. She was tired, always tired. And lately she was worried too. The hospital where she worked was cutting staff. It seemed each day fewer people were expected to do more work. It was like trying to climb a mountain that keeps getting taller as you go. Mom was forty-four, but just yesterday she said, "I'm like an old car that's run out of warranty, baby. You know what happens then. Old car is ready for the junk heap. Well, maybe that hospital is gonna tell me one of these days—'Mattie Mae Wills, we don't need you anymore. We can get somebody younger and cheaper.'"

"Mom, you're not old at all," Darcy had said, but they were only words, empty words. They could not erase the dark, weary lines from beneath her mother's eyes.

Darcy headed down the street toward Bluford High School. It was not a terrible neighborhood they lived in; it just was not good. Many front yards were not cared for. Debris—fast food wrappers, plastic bags, old newspapers—blew around and piled against fences and curbs. Darcy hated that. Sometimes she and other kids from school spent Saturday mornings cleaning up, but it seemed a losing battle. Now, as she walked, she tried to focus on small spots of beauty along the way. Mrs. Walker's pink and white roses bobbed proudly in the morning breeze. The Hustons' rock garden was carefully designed around a wooden windmill.

As she neared Bluford, Darcy thought about the science project that her biology teacher, Ms. Reed, was assigning. Darcy was doing hers on tidal pools. She was looking forward to visiting a real tidal pool, taking pictures, and doing research. Today, Ms. Reed would be dividing the students into teams of two. Darcy wanted to be paired with her close friend, Brisana Meeks. They were both excellent students, a cut above most kids at Bluford, Darcy thought.

"Today, we are forming project teams so that each student can gain something valuable from the other," Ms. Reed said as Darcy sat at her desk. Ms. Reed was a tall, stately woman who reminded Darcy of the Statue of Liberty. She would have been a perfect model for the statue if Lady Liberty had been a black woman. She never would have been called pretty, but it was possible she might have been called a handsome woman. "For this assignment, each of you will be working with someone you've never worked with before."

Darcy was worried. If she was not teamed with Brisana,

maybe she would be teamed with some really dumb student who would pull her down. Darcy was a little ashamed of herself for thinking that way. Grandma used to say that all flowers are equal, but different. The simple daisy was just as lovely as the prize rose. But still Darcy did not want to be paired with some weak partner who would lower her grade.

"Darcy Wills will be teamed with Tarah Carson," Ms. Reed announced.

Darcy gasped. Not Tarah! Not that big, chunky girl with the brassy voice who squeezed herself into tight skirts and wore lime green or hot pink satin tops and cheap jewelry. Not Tarah who hung out with Cooper Hodden, that loser who was barely hanging on to his football eligibility. Darcy had heard that Cooper had been left back once or twice and even got his driver's license as a sophomore. Darcy's face felt hot with anger. Why was Ms. Reed doing this?

Hakeem Randall, a handsome, shy boy who sat in the back row, was teamed with the class blabbermouth, LaShawn Appleby. Darcy had a secret crush on Hakeem since freshman year. So far she had only shared this with her diary, never with another living soul.

It was almost as though Ms. Reed was playing some devilish game. Darcy glanced at Tarah, who was smiling broadly. Tarah had an enormous smile, and her teeth contrasted harshly with her dark red lipstick. "Great," Darcy muttered under her breath.

Ms. Reed ordered the teams to meet so they could begin to plan their projects.

As she sat down by Tarah, Darcy was instantly sickened by a syrupy-sweet odor.

She must have doused herself with cheap perfume this morning , Darcy thought.

"Hey, girl," Tarah said. "Well, don't you look down in the mouth. What's got you lookin' that way?"

It was hard for Darcy to meet new people, especially someone like Tarah, a person Aunt Charlotte would call "low class." These were people who were loud and rude. They drank too much, used drugs, got into fights and ruined the neighborhood. They yelled ugly insults at people, even at their friends. Darcy did not actually know that Tarah did anything like this personally, but she seemed like the type who did.

"I just didn't think you'd be interested in tidal pools," Darcy explained.

Tarah slammed her big hand on the desk, making her gold bracelets jangle like ice cubes in a glass, and laughed. Darcy had never heard a mule bray, but she was sure it made exactly the same sound. Then Tarah leaned close and whispered, "Girl, I don't know a tidal pool from a fool. Ms. Reed stuck us together to mess with our heads, you hear what I'm sayin'?"

"Maybe we could switch to other partners," Darcy said nervously.

A big smile spread slowly over Tarah's face. "Nah, I think I'm gonna enjoy this. You're always sittin' here like a princess collecting your A's. Now you gotta work with a regular person, so you better loosen up, girl!"

Darcy felt as if her teeth were glued to her tongue. She fumbled in her bag for her outline of the project. It all seemed like a horrible joke now. She and Tarah Carson standing knee-deep in the muck of a tidal pool!

"Worms live there, don't they?" Tarah asked, twisting a big gold ring on her chubby finger.

"Yeah, I guess," Darcy replied.

"Big green worms," Tarah continued. "So if you get your feet stuck in the bottom of that old tidal pool, and you can't get out, do the worms crawl up your clothes?"

Darcy ignored the remark. "I'd like for us to go there soon, you know, look around."

"My boyfriend, Cooper, he goes down to the ocean all the time. He can take us. He says he's seen these fiddler crabs. They look like big spiders, and they'll try to bite your toes off. Cooper says so," Tarah said.

"Stop being silly," Darcy shot back. "If you' re not even going to be serious . . . "

"You think you're better than me, don't you?" Tarah suddenly growled.

"I never said—" Darcy blurted.

"You don't have to say it, girl. It's in your eyes. You think I'm a low-life and you're something special. Well, I got more friends than you got fingers and toes together. You got no friends, and everybody laughs at you behind your back. Know what the word on you is? Darcy Wills give you the chills."

Just then, the bell rang, and Darcy was glad for the excuse to turn away from Tarah, to hide the hot tears welling in her eyes. She quickly rushed from the classroom, relieved that school was over. Darcy did not think she could bear to sit through another class just now.

Darcy headed down the long street towards home. She did not like Tarah. Maybe it was wrong, but it was true. Still, Tarah's brutal words hurt. Even stupid, awful people might tell you the truth about yourself. And Darcy did not have any real friends, except for Brisana. Maybe the other kids were mocking her behind her back. Darcy was very slender, not as shapely as many of the other girls. She remembered the time when Cooper Hodden was hanging in front of the deli with his friends, and he yelled as Darcy went by, "Hey, is that really a female there? Sure don't look like it. Looks more like an old broomstick with hair. " His companions laughed rudely, and Darcy had walked a little faster.

A terrible thought clawed at Darcy. Maybe she was the loser, not Tarah. Tarah was always hanging with a bunch of kids, laughing and joking. She would go down the hall to the lockers and greetings would come from everywhere. "Hey, Tarah!" "What's up, Tar?" "See ya at lunch, girl." When Darcy went to the lockers, there was dead silence.

Darcy usually glanced into stores on her way home from school. She enjoyed looking at the trays of chicken feet and pork ears at the little Asian grocery store. Sometimes she would even steal a glance at the diners sitting by the picture window at the Golden Grill Restaurant. But today she stare d straight ahead, her shoulders drooping.

If this had happened last year, she would have gone directly to Grandma's house, a block from where Darcy lived. How many times had Darcy and Jamee run to Grandma's, eaten applesauce cookies, drunk cider, and poured out their troubles to Grandma. Somehow, their problems would always dissolve in the warmth of her love and wisdom. But now Grandma was a frail figure in the corner of their apartment, saying little. And what little she did say made less and less sense.

Darcy was usually the first one home. The minute she got there, Mom left for the hospital to take the 3:00 to 11:00 shift in the ER. By the time Mom finished her paperwork at the hospital, she would be lucky to be home again by midnight. After Mom left, Darcy went to Grandma's room to give her the malted nutrition drink that the doctor ordered her to have three times a day.

"Want to drink your chocolate malt, Grandma?" Darcy asked, pulling up a chair beside Grandma's bed.

Grandma was sitting up, and her eyes were open. "No. I'm not hungry," she said listlessly. She always said that.

"You need to drink your malt, Grandma," Darcy insisted, gently putting the straw between the pinched lips.

Grandma sucked the malt slowly. "Grandma, nobody likes me at school," Darcy said. She did not expect any response. But there was a strange comfort in telling Grandma anyway. "Everybody laughs at me. It's because I'm shy and maybe stuck-up, too, I guess. But I don't mean to be. Stuck-up, I mean. Maybe I'm weird. I could be weird, I guess. I could be like Aunt Charlotte . . ." Tears rolled down Darcy's cheeks. Her heart ached with loneliness. There was nobody to talk to anymore, nobody who had time to listen, nobody who understood.

Grandma blinked and pushed the straw away. Her eyes brightened as they did now and then. "You are a wonderful girl. Everybody knows that," Grandma said in an almost normal voice. It happened like that sometimes. It was like being in the middle of a dark storm and having the clouds part, revealing a patch of clear, sunlit blue. For just a few precious minutes, Grandma was bright-eyed and saying normal things.

"Oh, Grandma, I'm so lonely," Darcy cried, pressing her head against Grandma's small shoulder.

"You were such a beautiful baby," Grandma said, stroking her hair." 'That one is going to shine like the morning star.' That's what I told your Mama. 'That child is going to shine like the morning star.' Tell me, Angelcake, is your daddy home yet?"

Darcy straightened. "Not yet." Her heart pounded so hard, she could feel it thumping in her chest. Darcy's father had not been home in five years.

"Well, tell him to see me when he gets home. I want him to buy you that blue dress you liked in the store window. That's for you, Angelcake. Tell him I've got money. My social security came, you know. I have money for the blue dress," Grandma said, her eyes slipping shut.

Just then, Darcy heard the apartment door slam. Jamee had come home. Now she stood in the hall, her hands belligerently on her hips. "Are you talking to Grandma again?" Jamee demanded.

"She was talking like normal," Darcy said. "Sometimes she does. You know she does."

"That is so stupid," Jamee snapped. "She never says anything right anymore. Not anything!" Jamee's voice trembled.

Darcy got up quickly and set down the can of malted milk. She ran to Jamee and put her arms around her sister. "Jamee, I know you're hurting too."

"Oh, don't be stupid," Jamee protested, but Darcy hugged her more tightly, and in a few seconds Jamee was crying. "She was the best thing in this stupid house," Jamee cried. "Why'd she have to go?"

"She didn't go," Darcy said. "Not really."

"She did! She did!" Jamee sobbed. She struggled free of Darcy, ran to her room, and slammed the door. In a minute, Darcy heard the bone-rattling sound of rap music.

Lost and Found, a Bluford Series™ novel, is reprinted with permission from Townsend Press. Copyright © 2002.

Want to read more? This and other Bluford Series™ novels and paperbacks can be purchased for $1 each at www.townsendpress.com.

Teens:
How to Get More Out of This Book

Self-help: The teens who wrote the stories in this book did so because they hope that telling their stories will help readers who are facing similar challenges. They want you to know that you are not alone, and that taking specific steps can help you manage or overcome very difficult situations. They've done their best to be clear about the actions that worked for them so you can see if they'll work for you.

Writing: You can also use the book to improve your writing skills. Each teen in this book wrote 5-10 drafts of his or her story before it was published. If you read the stories closely you'll see that the teens work to include a beginning, a middle, and an end, and good scenes, description, dialogue, and anecdotes (little stories). To improve your writing, take a look at how these writers construct their stories. Try some of their techniques in your own writing.

Reading: Finally, you'll notice that we include the first chapter from a Bluford Series novel in this book, alongside the true stories by teens. We hope you'll like it enough to continue reading. The more you read, the more you'll strengthen your reading skills. Teens at Youth Communication like the Bluford novels because they explore themes similar to those in their own stories. Your school may already have the Bluford books. If not, you can order them online for only $1.

Resources on the Web

We will occasionally post Think About It questions on our website, www.youthcomm.org, to accompany stories in this and other Youth Communication books. We try out the questions with teens and post the ones they like best. Many teens report that writing answers to those questions in a journal is very helpful.

How to Use This Book in Staff Training

Staff say that reading these stories gives them greater insight into what teens are thinking and feeling, and new strategies for working with them. You can help the staff you work with by using these stories as case studies.

Select one story to read in the group, and ask staff to identify and discuss the main issue facing the teen. There may be disagreement about this, based on the background and experience of staff. That is fine. One point of the exercise is that teens have complex lives and needs. Adults can probably be more effective if they don't focus too narrowly and can see several dimensions of their clients.

Ask staff: What issues or feelings does the story provoke in them? What kind of help do they think the teen wants? What interventions are likely to be most promising? Least effective? Why? How would you build trust with the teen writer? How have other adults failed the teen, and how might that affect his or her willingness to accept help? What other resources would be helpful to this teen, such as peer support, a mentor, counseling, family therapy, etc.

Resources on the Web

From time to time we will post Think About It questions on our website, www.youthcomm.org, to accompany stories in this and other Youth Communication books. We try out the questions with teens and post the ones that they find most effective. We'll also post lesson for some of the stories. Adults can use the questions and lessons in workshops.

Discussion Guide

Teachers and Staff:
How to Use This Book in Groups

When working with teens individually or in groups, you can use these stories can help young people face difficult issues in a way that feels safe to them. That's because talking about the issues in the stories usually feels safer to teens than talking about those same issues in their own lives. Addressing issues through the stories allows for some personal distance; they hit close to home, but not too close. Talking about them opens up a safe place for reflection. As teens gain confidence talking about the issues in the stories, they usually become more comfortable talking about those issues in their own lives.

Below are general questions to guide your discussion. In most cases you can read a story and conduct a discussion in one 45-minute session. Teens are usually happy to read the stories aloud, with each teen reading a paragraph or two. (Allow teens to pass if they don't want to read.) It takes 10-15 minutes to read a story straight through. However, it is often more effective to let workshop participants make comments and discuss the story as you go along. The workshop leader may even want to annotate her copy of the story beforehand with key questions.

If teens read the story ahead of time or silently, it's good to break the ice with a few questions that get everyone on the same page: Who is the main character? How old is she? What happened to her? How did she respond? Another good starting question is: "What stood out for you in the story?" Go around the room and let each person briefly mention one thing.

Then move on to open-ended questions, which encourage participants to think more deeply about what the writers were feeling, the choices they faced, and they actions they took. There are no right or wrong answers to the open-ended questions.

Open-ended questions encourage participants to think about how the themes, emotions, and choices in the stories relate to their own lives. Here are some examples of open-ended questions that we have found to be effective. You can use variations of these questions with almost any story in this book.

—What main problem or challenge did the writer face?

—What choices did the teen have in trying to deal with the problem?

—Which way of dealing with the problem was most effective for the teen? Why?

—What strengths, skills, or resources did the teen use to address the challenge?

—If you were in the writer's shoes, what would you have done?

—What could adults have done better to help this young person?

—What have you learned by reading this story that you didn't know before?

—What, if anything, will you do differently after reading this story?

—What surprised you in this story?

—Do you have a different view of this issue, or see a different way of dealing with it, after reading this story? Why or why not?

Credits

The stories in this book originally appeared in the following Youth Communication publications:

"My First Day," by Tamecka Crawford, *Represent*, September/October 1993; "At Home in the Group Home," by Taheerah Mahdi, *Represent*, September/October 2003; "Get Me Outta Here!" by Miguel Ayala, *New Youth Connections*, September/October 2003; "The Rules Make Me Feel Safe," by Angela R., *Represent*, January/February 1995; "The Adventure Begins," by Delicia Jones, *Represent*, March/April 2000; "I'll Take the System," by Erica Harrigan, *Represent*, November/December 2004; "All the Lonely People," by Karol Kwiatkowska, *Represent*, November/December 2000; "Trapped!" by Mariah Lopez, *Represent*, January/February 2000; "Can the Counselors Keep a Secret?" by Anonymous, *Represent*, January/February 1995; "Making It on My Own," by Eric Edmonson, *Represent*, March/April 1999; "Sober in a World of Unreality," by Charlene Carter, *Represent*, September/October 2000; "No One To Trust," by Lenny Jones, *Represent*, November/December 1995; "Safety in Numbers," by Ja'Nelle Earle, *Represent*, July/August 2002; "Snow White," by Karol Kwiatkowska, *Represent*, November/December 2000; "Overcoming My Fear of Gays," by Sharif Berkeley, *Represent*, January/February 1996; "Fight for Your Respect" by Anonymous, *Represent*, July/August 1997; "Jasmine, the Scapegoat," by Angela R., *Represent*, November/December 1994; "Girls Like Me," by Rana Sino, *Represent*, September/October 2003; "Five Steps Behind," by Kareem Banks, *Represent*, January/February 2007; "Man With a Plan," by Michael Orr, *New Youth Connections*, January/February 2007; "Missing My Old Group Home," by Max Moran, *Represent*, May/June 1996.

About
Youth Communication

Youth Communication, founded in 1980, is a nonprofit youth development program located in New York City whose mission is to teach writing, journalism, and leadership skills. The teenagers we train become writers for our websites and books and for two print magazines: *New Youth Connections*, a general-interest youth magazine, and *Represent*, a magazine by and for young people in foster care.

Each year, up to 100 young people participate in Youth Communication's school-year and summer journalism workshops, where they work under the direction of full-time professional editors. Most are African-American, Latino, or Asian, and many are recent immigrants. The opportunity to reach their peers with accurate portrayals of their lives and important self-help information motivates the young writers to create powerful stories.

Our goal is to run a strong youth development program in which teens produce high quality stories that inform and inspire their peers. Doing so requires us to be sensitive to the complicated lives and emotions of the teen participants while also providing an intellectually rigorous experience. We achieve that goal in the writing/teaching/editing relationship, which is the core of our program.

Our teaching and editorial process begins with discussions

between adult editors and the teen staff. In those meetings, the teens and the editors work together to identify the most important issues in the teens' lives and to figure out how those issues can be turned into stories that will resonate with teen readers.

Once story topics are chosen, students begin the process of crafting their stories. For a personal story, that means revisiting events in one's past to understand their significance for the future. For a commentary, it means developing a logical and persuasive point of view. For a reported story, it means gathering information through research and interviews. Students look inward and outward as they try to make sense of their experiences and the world around them and find the points of intersection between personal and social concerns. That process can take a few weeks or a few months. Stories frequently go through ten or more drafts as students work under the guidance of their editors, the way any professional writer does.

Many of the students who walk through our doors have uneven skills, as a result of poor education, living under extremely stressful conditions, or coming from homes where English is a second language. Yet, to complete their stories, students must successfully perform a wide range of activities, including writing and rewriting, reading, discussion, reflection, research, interviewing, and typing. They must work as members of a team and they must accept individual responsibility. They learn to provide constructive criticism, and to accept it. They engage in explorations of truthfulness, fairness, and accuracy. They meet deadlines. They must develop the audacity to believe that they have something important to say and the humility to recognize that saying it well is not a process of instant gratification. Rather, it usually requires a long, hard struggle through many discussions and much rewriting.

It would be impossible to teach these skills and dispositions as separate, disconnected topics, like grammar, ethics, or assertiveness. However, we find that students make rapid progress when they are learning skills in the context of an inquiry that is personally significant to them and that will benefit their peers.

When teens publish their stories—in *New Youth Connections* and *Represent*, on the web, and in other publications—they reach tens of thousands of teen and adult readers. Teachers, counselors, social workers, and other adults circulate the stories to young people in their classes and out-of-school youth programs. Adults tell us that teens in their programs—including many who are ordinarily resistant to reading—clamor for the stories. Teen readers report that the stories give them information they can't get anywhere else, and inspire them to reflect on their lives and open lines of communication with adults.

Writers usually participate in our program for one semester, though some stay much longer. Years later, many of them report that working here was a turning point in their lives—that it helped them acquire the confidence and skills that they needed for success in college and careers. Scores of our graduates have overcome tremendous obstacles to become journalists, writers, and novelists. They include National Book Award finalist and MacArthur Fellowship winner Edwidge Danticat, novelist Ernesto Quinonez, writer Veronica Chambers, and *New York Times* reporter Rachel Swarns. Hundreds more are working in law, business, and other careers. Many are teachers, principals, and youth workers, and several have started nonprofit youth programs themselves and work as mentors—helping another generation of young people develop their skills and find their voices.

Youth Communication is a nonprofit educational corporation. Contributions are gratefully accepted and are tax deductible to the fullest extent of the law.

To make a contribution, or for information about our publications and programs, including our catalog of over 100 books and curricula for hard-to-reach teens, see www.youthcomm.org

About The Editors

Al Desetta has been an editor of Youth Communication's two teen magazines, *Foster Care Youth United* (now known as *Represent*) and *New Youth Connections*. He was also an instructor in Youth Communication's juvenile prison writing program. In 1991, he became the organization's first director of teacher development, working with high school teachers to help them produce better writers and student publications.

Prior to working at Youth Communication, Desetta directed environmental education projects in New York City public high schools and worked as a reporter.

He has a master's degree in English literature from City College of the City University of New York and a bachelor's degree from the State University of New York at Binghamton, and he was a Revson Fellow at Columbia University for the 1990-91 academic year.

He is the editor of many books, including several other Youth Communication anthologies: *The Heart Knows Something Different: Teenage Voices from the Foster Care System*, *The Struggle to Be Strong*, and *The Courage to Be Yourself*. He is currently a freelance editor.

Keith Hefner co-founded Youth Communication in 1980 and has directed it ever since. He is the recipient of the Luther P. Jackson Education Award from the New York Association of Black Journalists and a MacArthur Fellowship. He was also a Revson Fellow at Columbia University.

Laura Longhine is the editorial director at Youth Communication. She edited *Represent*, Youth Communication's magazine by and for youth in foster care, for three years, and has written for a variety of publications. She has a BA in English from Tufts University and an MS in Journalism from Columbia University.

More Helpful Books
From Youth Communication

Do You Have What It Takes? A Comprehensive Guide to Success After Foster Care. In this survival manual, current and former foster teens show how they prepared not only for the practical challenges they've faced on the road to independence, but also the emotional ones. Worksheets and exercises help foster teens plan for their future. Activity pages at the end of each chapter help social workers, independent living instructors, and other leaders use the stories with individuals or in groups. (Youth Communication)

The Struggle to Be Strong: True Stories by Teens About Overcoming Tough Times. Foreword by Veronica Chambers. Help young people identify and build on their own strengths with 30 personal stories about resiliency. (Free Spirit)

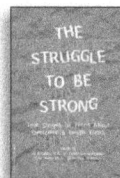

Depression, Anger, Sadness: Teens Write About Facing Difficult Emotions. Give teens the confidence they need to seek help when they need it. These teens write candidly about difficult emotional problems—such as depression, cutting, and domestic violence—and how they have tried to help themselves. (Youth Communication)

What Staff Need to Know: Teens Write About What Works. How can foster parents, group home staff, caseworkers, social workers, and teachers best help teens? These stories show how communication can be improved on both sides, and provide insight into what kinds of approaches and styles work best. (Youth Communication)

Out of the Shadows: Teens Write About Surviving Sexual Abuse. Help teens feel less alone and more hopeful about overcoming the trauma of sexual abuse. This collection includes first-person accounts by male and female survivors grappling with fear, shame, and guilt. (Youth Communication)

Just the Two of Us: Teens Write About Building Good Relationships. Show teens how to make and maintain healthy relationships (and avoid bad ones). Many teens in care have had poor role models and are emotionally vulnerable. These stories demonstrate good and bad choices teens make in friendship and romance. (Youth Communication)

The Fury Inside: Teens Write About Anger. Help teens manage their anger. These writers show how they got better control of their emotions and sought the support of others. (Youth Communication)

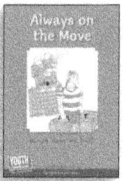

Always on the Move: Teens Write About Changing Homes and Staff. Help teens feel less alone with these stories about how their peers have coped with the painful experience of frequent placement changes, and turnover among staff and social workers. (Youth Communication)

Two Moms in My Heart: Teens Write About the Adoption Option. Teens will appreciate these stories by peers who describe how complicated the adoption experience can be—even when it should give them a more stable home than foster care. (Youth Communication)

My Secret Addiction: Teens Write About Cutting. These true accounts of cutting, or self-mutilation, offer a window into the personal and family situations that lead to this secret habit, and show how teens can get the help they need. (Youth Communication)

Growing Up Together: Teens Write About Being Parents. Give teens a realistic view of the conflicts and burdens of parenthood with these stories from real teen parents. The stories also reveal how teens grew as individuals by struggling to become responsible parents. (Youth Communication)

To order these and other books, go to:
www.youthcomm.org
or call 212-279-0708 x115